LIGHT *at the* END *of the* FUNNEL

DANIELLE FITZPATRICK CLARK

Light at the End of the Funnel

Copyright © 2019 by Danielle Fitzpatrick Clark
ISBN: 978-0-578-59074-5

TABLE OF CONTENTS

FOREWORD

By: Danielle Fitzpatrick Clark

Entrepreneurship isn't a destination. It isn't sexy or romantic either. It's work, blood, sweat and tears. It takes patience, grit and some days, bottomless cups of coffee.

Some will say, "entrepreneurship just isn't for me."

And then there are others who say, "I couldn't live any other way."

This book is about the latter. This is a book full of the dreamers, the doers, the innovators, and the creatives who are looking to make a difference.

Who are looking for solutions to what just doesn't make sense in the world we live in today. Who are looking to make a difference.

This book is the solution to a bigger problem in the entrepreneurial industry. Being in the online marketing world for over a decade, there's been a progression of sorts. The best sales and marketing gurus get the clients. It's caused many who are entering the digital world to 'up their game' in an effort to keep up with the rat race.

Which leads to marketing traps like…

"Learn how I launch my course and earned 6-figures in 3 days."

"I was the best kept secret 7-days ago and with this one simple hack I've created thousands of new sign ups to my email list."

Or my personal favorite…

"Build your 7-figure funnel in 30 days or less."

Those who aren't comfortable playing the 'sales' game are left scratching their heads, second guessing their abilities, and thinking, "what am I doing wrong?"

If you've been there or are currently there, I've got some good news for you.

YOU'RE NOT DOING ANYTHING WRONG!

Online marketing has been designed much like the filters on our smart phones. Only the good stuff shows up. Most of the posts you see in the online space, bragging about the successes are leaving out the juiciest parts. THE FAILURES.

The, 'falling flat on your face, get off your knees, wipe the dust off and keep going,' moments! And those are the moments that are sink or swim, fight or flight, do or die. Those are the moment you get to decide whether you're failing forward or simply failing. By simply acknowledging the tough moments, you give rise and permission for others to do the same.

That's exactly what this group of authors will do for you in this edition of Light at the End of the Funnel. Grab your notebook, give yourself a good hour to read through the stories, and have your smart phone close by so you can scan the author's QR codes to learn more about them, connect with them personally, and receive massive value beyond the book.

Until then, keep shining your light and leave some beauty wherever you may go.

Danielle Fitzpatrick Clark

Danielle Fitzpatrick Clark
Founder and CEO of Influence Builder
Producer of Light at the End of the Funnel Book Series

INTEGRATION FOR GREATER IMPACT

By Danielle Fitzpatrick Clark

Can you share a moment in your entrepreneurial journey that was a huge Ah-Ha and gamechanger?

I remember it clearly. It was the day I literally dropped to my knees and screamed, "I can't take it anymore…"

A little dramatic? Perhaps, and *eye opening.*

It was a Friday, and the morning had started insanely busy. My two oldest daughters needed help getting ready for school, my husband needed his shirt ironed for work, and the one-year old was wanting cuddles and comfort after coming off a nasty cold. On top of all that, it was only 7:30am in the morning and I already had fifteen emails that had been sent the night before around midnight from 3 different clients wanting work done by noon that same day.

I had thirty minutes to get my two oldest and the husband out the door, all with daughter number three on my hip as I made lunches, packed bookbags, filled water bottles, and gathered up shoes and socks for everyone. That morning, my husband went to work with a little more wrinkle in his shirt, because well...priorities. I felt a surge of guilt as I told him I wouldn't be able to iron his shirt like I had promised the night before. I hate breaking promises.

Everyone made it out the door on time, and my youngest and I were ready for breakfast and email replies. I felt a lump in my throat as I read through the fifteen client emails.

The common theme with all emails was, "I want more." Two of the clients wanted to increase the scope of work and include it within the parameters of payments we had already finalized. So, more work, no more money. Another client wanted to shift everything in her business plan and wanted an emergency team meeting that morning to go over the new direction of her company.

As I read through each email the hairs on the back of my arms started to stand up, and stress and anxiety soon took over my body as I came to the realization, "I'm going to have to work another weekend."

The thought of working another weekend, after eight months of working in my business 80+ hours per week was heart breaking. I wanted to spend time with my family! I needed uninterrupted time, that didn't require an emergency client call or fixing a website glitch or putting out another fire. That was THE LAST THING I wanted to do this upcoming weekend, a weekend I had promised myself I would take off to rest and rejuvenate. Yet, the people-pleaser in me didn't feel like there was another choice, especially if I wanted to keep my clients happy. My family would forgive me, but I wasn't so sure my clients would.

As the tears started to surge into my exhausted and overstrained eyes, I picked my youngest up from her highchair and placed her in the activity walker, so I could take a moment. I felt dizzy and short of breath as I walked into my bedroom and closed the door…and dropped to my knees.

The past eight months flashed before my eyes, as the tears rolled down my cheeks…It wasn't just one moment, or one client, or one negative incident. It was the accumulation of small moments, unideal clients, inauthentic conversations, and lackluster success and growth that finally made me snap and fall. The metaphorical "rock bottom" is exactly what I hit. Up until that point I had convinced myself that moments like this didn't exist. How could anyone let themselves hit rock bottom?

As I kneeled in my bedroom, door locked, ugly crying and sobbing, my negative self-talk kicked up into high gear. I was consumed with feelings of misery and seclusion, of hopelessness and unfulfillment, and both emotionally and physically I felt like a doormat that had been stampeded by a herd of wild buffalo. I knew that I couldn't keep going the way I was going. I knew

···

I couldn't keep running my business as a
PEOPLE-PLEASING SIDEKICK
in my own hero story

···

and I knew I couldn't keep saying yes to ALL the clients who wanted to work with me, when deep down I knew it wasn't a good fit for MANY of them.

With that realization, the negative self-talk slowly subsided, the tension that had settled in my chest eased, and I could breathe a little more slowly. Deep down, I realized what I wanted. I realized the time was NOW to transform who I was into who I most wanted to be. I saw a much stronger person within, a leader, an innovator, and a person who had gifts and a message to share with the world.

After that moment in my bedroom, the tears dwindled, I stood up, wiped my face, and unlocked my door, and went back to being mom, wife, and business owner with a new-found energy that everything was going to change from this day forward.

While I wanted to have immediate change, I knew small, incremental changes were needed for me to have lasting results. That day my small change was to take my first weekend off in months. I decided that to speed up, I needed to first slow down.

I also decided I needed to start seeing myself for the expert I truly was, and for the value I brought. For all the clients I had, and the businesses I had helped build to six- and seven-figures, I knew my knowledge and perspective in the industry was absolutely needed and wanted. The best way to do that was to coach and consult others and take on a larger role that would bring me out from behind the curtains, and in front of my ideal clients. Now, I work with mission-based, heart-centered entrepreneurs and business owners, the ones who are driven by something greater than themselves or the money, people who give back.

How did you persevere during this moment?

Perseverance came in the form of release and gratitude after I made the decision that change was necessary for me to create a life and business that I loved. I knew that everything first and foremost had to start with me because I was creating my own reality.

What I soon discovered was my lack of self-love and acceptance, and my current life was a direct reflection of that. I was working with clients I didn't love, taking on projects with continuous scope creep, and keeping myself hidden behind the scenes because

I didn't feel GOOD *enough,* FUNNY *enough, or that my words weren't* THOUGHT-PROVOKING *enough to make the impact I wanted to make.*

This realization brought feelings ranging from guilt and shame all the way to happiness and excitement. I was confused, uncomfortable, and hopeful. I kept identifying my feelings every day, taking more and more time to myself, and finding more and more areas of to be grateful for in my life and business.

I ended up quitting a very lucrative contract and wrapping up relationships with several clients I no longer felt compelled to work with, all within a two-week period of my initial drop-to-my-knees, rock bottom moment. I went from eight clients to two almost overnight.

To the untrained eye, I was committing financial suicide, and would be closing my business if I wasn't able to find new clients. For the clients I did keep, I appreciated them and showered them with gratitude. The funny thing was, they weren't used to hearing praise and recognition from their contractors, and they put out a few emails recommending me to their peers. Several of those peers hired me immediately. Not only were they fantastic new clients, they were exactly the type of clients I loved. They were looking for help with strategy and scaling, giving me an opportunity to coach them into six-figure success and beyond.

With every new client came new possibilities and growth, and with this growth came more opportunities for gratitude.

Even better, I attracted people who understood what I was going through, people who had been there before me and had found ways to change their inner game to have a better outer experience. This was just the start of me stepping into the person I truly was meant to be, and the support came to me seamlessly.

What did you learn from the experience?

This experience created three big takeaways for me. The first major takeaway was the power in being present and taking notice of my thoughts and feelings. As an expert in so many areas of online marketing and technology, and with a client roster so dependent on my abilities, I often found myself going through the motions, getting the job done, and pushing aside my creativity, which ultimately left me feeling hollow and without joy and pride in the work I was doing. I was accomplishing so much yet feeling so little fulfillment.

When something doesn't feel right, that's a clear indication to stop and take a long hard look at what you're doing. Many of us push through, bury our heads in the sand, and don't come up for air until we feel comfortable to do so. Eventually, I found that logic only takes you so far in any business, and

....

there's a massive need for **CREATIVITY**
in your work.

....

While logic is the vehicle you use to drive action, creativity is the map that will take you to your destination.

Part of what becomes uncomfortable in business is not trusting yourself with your creativity and how it will bring you to the outcome you truly desire. This is where I see entrepreneurs and business owners jump on the hamster wheel for weeks, months, and, in some cases, years. Instead of trusting themselves, and creating their own map, they follow someone else's. Then they become frustrated with their lackluster results, and cycle over and over trying to find the answer in someone else, or some other program or course.

For example, one of my clients came to me for marketing help. Up until that time she had spent thousands of dollars on programs, masterminds, and courses, and still had not sold any product or service in her business. When we dug in to her business a little she discovered that she had been following what she was being taught so closely that she didn't take a step back to see who her ideal clients were and what they needed. In four weeks of working together, she made $5,000 in product sales.

This client had to take a step back from what others were teaching her so she could find her own path. I find this in many of my clients, and a simple mindset shift can take them where they want to go. If they would allow themselves to become uncomfortable with the unknown so they can find comfort in themselves, they will find results and growth will appear quickly and easily in their business.

The second takeaway is the concept of comfort. Here's what I learned about being comfortable…it's more uncomfortable and unhealthy in the long run to stick with what feels safe in your business than it is to

step outside the box and try something
NEW *and* INTIMIDATING.

Here's a real-life example: for those of you who have kids, think about the times they scrape their knees. It's bleeding, raw, and they are screaming and writhing in pain, yet when you pull out the peroxide, ointment, and gauze, they freak out and beg you to just use a Band-Aid. Why is that? Because they do not want to feel the initial pain of cleaning their scrape before putting on the Band-Aid and ointment for better healing. It's the initial pain that keeps them from avoiding the good healing. Here is the thing about wounds: when they go uncleaned, they get infected, and cause more pain, more misery, and, in some cases, hospital visits, which end up costing more time, more money, and more overall discomfort.

Let's not even go into the whole "ripping off the Band-Aid" procedure versus slowly tearing it off!

Back to my experience in my business and life, I have found the initial pain and discomfort of change is often a deterrent for self-reflection and growth.

Which brings me to my third learning point from this experience... avoidance. I've practiced avoidance, the avoidance of crucial shifts in my business, of crucial conversations with clients, and crucial discussions with myself and the promises I've kept for myself and the promises I've sorely broken. The more I avoid, push aside, or hide from a problem, the further I get from a solution, and not just any solution, but the solution that will ultimately give me a greater sense of peace and accomplishment in my business. My first year of coaching and consulting is an example of this.

I had spent much of the year creating a massive following, and at the end of the year I had reached a following of over 22,000 on social media and email. Yet, I had avoided looking at my schedule and how much time I was spending in my business and the time that was spending with my family. What you resist often persists, and I was exhausted, overworked, and heading towards burn out. What I had avoided became unavoidable, and

I had to take steps toward working **SMARTER,** *with fewer hours,*

and needed to build a team to do so. In the end, what I had avoided was exactly what I needed to scale my business quickly.

What did you learn about yourself from this experience?

The best part of entrepreneurship is that we all have experiences that make us unique and valuable and perfect for not only our ideal clients, but for our *dream* clients.

What I've learned is that **TRANSFORMATION** *is possible for* **ANYONE** who is willing and ready, for anyone who will look at their life, as it is today, and own every piece of it. When you take steps to transform from the inside out, you'll find that the ups and downs of entrepreneurship can be worked through easily, and with a solution that makes sense. Success always follows when you focus on finding a solution.

When I looked at my clients, the ones who were making a six- or seven-figure profit in their business had two things in common: emotional intelligence and resiliency. Their years of experience had given them resiliency and being able to work with their emotions gave them intelligence and unwavering commitment.

With this knowledge, I learned how much I had been disempowering myself, losing who I was inside, and sacrificing my happiness because I just thought that was the way things were when you were "adulting." I thought that my experiences weren't my own, and they weren't within my control. During my Ah-Ha moment, I gave myself permission to understand and own the fact that I wasn't a victim, the universe and the people in it weren't conspiring against me, and it was just the opposite. Everything was happening for me and for my personal betterment.

I learned that not only am I meaningful, I am worthy of everything that life has to offer. I am a beacon of light for others who are seeking community within their entrepreneurial journey, and that to empower others I must first empower myself. I learned that the journey of self-discovery is one of the highest honors we as humans have on this incredible earth. I learned that anything is possible, and the first step is to recognize the possibilities within, and to take on the world even if you're afraid…even if you're unsure…and to know that you are everything you need, and your power has always, and will always be, within you. This isn't something that can be taught in a book, or with another program, or forced on you by any coach. The path of emotional intelligence and resiliency is a choice, one you must choose first for yourself, and then seek those who can support you fully in that experience.

What do you believe are the most important characteristics and skills one must possess to have a successful life?

Openness and curiosity are the two characteristics I would identify as essential for a successful life. We are the most powerful when we've opened ourselves to greatness and released the barriers that are holding us down.

That isn't something that you can wish on yourself, and it doesn't happen overnight. Because it's within you first and foremost, the person who unlocks your potential fully -- is you. Have the curiosity to dig in deep, go into the dark and come out to the light, just like the metaphoric scraped knee. There may be tears, there may be pain, and yet both subside quickly when you nurture and clean the wound, so you can heal better.

For example, one of my clients came to me with a plan for the year halfway through the year, yet he wasn't thrilled about the business plan he had developed with his initial coach. Regardless, he still planned on following it. In our first session together, we discovered that the business plan wasn't his own, and he felt it had been created with someone else in mind. Instead of changing everything about the plan, we took out the activities he wasn't passionate about, and replaced them with other activities that excited him, and that he looked forward to starting and completing. He went on to have not only a successful year, but he doubled his income from the year before, all because he was open and curious to the possibilities in his business.

The skill of integration is key for overall success and happiness in life and in business. My definition of integration is a healthy balance between mind, body, and spirit, and an ability to notice and to listen to those aspects of yourself. Just as logic and brilliance can take you far in life, intuition and connectedness will take you further and in less time. Add in a healthy body functioning at peak performance, and you have a skillset and recipe for extraordinary success.

Integration has been one of the most essential skills to learn, and the most difficult. When I first started my business in 2009, I was all logic and intelligence. What I found was that I pushed and pushed to make things work for me in my business, yet nothing ended up working and I was completely unhappy. When I started to connect more with myself, my goals, my values, and my emotions, everything shifted for the better. I could see more opportunities that would help the growth of my business. I was able to connect more deeply with myself and found that my messaging became more relatable to my ideal clients, and I found that I was an incredible coach and consultant because I was able to laser focus on what my clients needed.

How do you use these skills and characteristics in your home, business and for your clients?

One of the first things I ask my clients to do before we do any type of mindset or business coaching is to first acknowledge their life and everything, they have brought into it. I ask them to think of everything they've experienced, all the moments they've categorized as good, and all the bad ones. I want them to consider the relationships they've had, and how they view themselves in these experiences. This is a time of release for most clients, a time for them to talk about all their worries, fears, and how they've viewed themselves as wrong in different ways. This can sometimes be an uncomfortable conversation, yet it has the biggest Ah-Ha moments that lead to immediate transformation for all my clients.

A client came to me and was completely overwhelmed and stressed in her business. It was bleeding into her life in several ways. We spent a good portion of our call chatting about what was going well and what wasn't going well in her life.

Finally, I asked, "Are you willing to take full and complete ownership of both the good and the bad?"

She responded with a hesitant, "I think so."

As we dug in a little deeper to the conversation, she discovered that many of the moments and experiences she identified has negative or bad, became the catalyst for those experiences she defined as good and even "amazing."

My client had discovered something special. Without the bad experiences, she would never had been motivated to take steps towards the good experiences, and so each bad experience was essential in her life. This simple technique of taking ownership of everything in your life is a way to take your power back, and to know that you and only you are in control of how you experience your life and business.

Many of the entrepreneurs I work with struggle with self-judgment and loathing in the time they spend working IN their business, and the time it takes away from their family and self-care. Yet,

....

their business is an **EXTENSION** *of them,*
their **EXPRESSION**, *and should be*
their **HAVEN** *for creativity.*

....

Once those judgments are released and they've taken ownership of everything they've defined as good *and* bad, my clients feel more open and curious about how to nurture themselves and find solutions within, rather than searching the internet for answers that are not meant for them. I call this **empowered decision making.**

Another client of mine came to me on the verge of complete and utter burnout. Her to-do list was a mile high, she had 25 clients depending on her, and she felt as though she were literally suffocating. In a short session, we discovered that she had been working IN her business, yet her business wasn't working FOR her. Since she wanted to maintain her schedule, instead of making massive changes, we simply integrated more quiet time outside in between client calls. She was able to commit to five minutes a day, and her business not only flourished, she flourished.

With integration comes balance, and with balance comes flow, and when business and life flow, opportunities arise, and when they arise, being present and aware will help you to capitalize on opportunities that are in alignment with who you are as an entrepreneur. They'll help you become a magnet for similar opportunities and dream clients.

Building momentum, creating a solid following, and focusing your time and energy on gratitude and service will lead to greater and greater impact.

By: Danielle Fitzpatrick Clark

Danielle is an international best-selling author, speaker and CEO of Influence Builder and Entrepreneur City Live events. She works with influencers and mission-based entrepreneurs to help them create impact, influence and powerful platforms. With over a decade of experience in online marketing, production and business strategy, she leads and supports 6-figure and 7-figure business owners in building their dream business, while creating their impact and leaving a lasting legacy in the world.

In between speaking gigs, production of bestselling books, and navigating her clients through implementing powerful marketing ecosystems for their business's foundational needs, you'll find Danielle playing with her three daughters, snuggling with her husband (co-author and co-host Erik Clark) and taming her own wild kingdom of pets in their home outside of Charlotte, NC.

FREE GIFT: *Ready to get more speaking gigs? Sign up for my next online challenge, "5 Speaking Gigs in 5 Days!"*

Scan me

THE POWER OF POSITIVE RELATIONSHIPS

By: Erik Clark

Can you share a moment in your entrepreneurial journey that was a huge Ah-Ha and gamechanger?

My biggest Ah-Ha moment was realizing how important relationships are to the success of my business. Starting out, I focused a lot of my time developing content (PowerPoint slides, sales decks, legal documents, etc.) and just assumed that clients would follow. Of course, this did not happen. I did everything I thought I was supposed to do and couldn't figure out why it wasn't working. I also couldn't figure out how some of the other entrepreneurs I knew were thriving without having some of fundamentals in place, or at least what I *thought* were the fundamentals. I knew they must be doing something that I wasn't, so I started observing these people during networking events and tried to figure out the secret to their success.

I started to notice that a couple of people closed a lot of work informally. The work wasn't *technically* sold; it's not like they were signing contracts on the spot. But handshakes were exchanged, and the deal was done. The formalities were settled later. Not everyone was doing this, or at least doing it well, but there were a few who were very successful. They were easy to point out during any event. They were usually the center of attention, at any event. They seemed to be having more interesting conversations than the ones going on around them.

I talked to them to see what they were doing that was so different and interesting. Over time, I realized they had made an effort to get to know me. They'd ask about how my business was going, how the family was, and might follow up on something that we had discussed during the last meeting. Nothing about their behavior was Earth-shattering or super-secret. It was something that took time and effort and, for whatever reason, most people at these events weren't willing to do it. At first, I wasn't either. It seemed like a lot of effort for people I may never see again, so at first it looked like a huge waste of time. You what's a bigger waste of time? Going to dozens of networking groups and blaming the group for not providing what you need.

Once I was able to see the bigger picture, I chose a couple groups and was a dedicated participant. I went to these groups every week. I got to know people and referred them to my friends and family. Once I started to participate, I began to reap the benefits. The meeting that was once a group of random people became colleagues and active participants in my success. I got leads from my groups, and some of these leads turned into sales.

My MARKETING *was being done for me*

and it was making my life so much easier. I was reciprocating by passing along dozens of leads and was sure to be as helpful as I could in making other people's businesses a success.

How did you persevere during this moment?

Preserving through this Ah-Ha moment was challenging. It meant that I had to change what I was doing and how I was doing it. I started by changing how I approached networking events. On the rare occasion I attended these events, I didn't fully engage with the participants. I would look for obvious business connections where we could immediately help each other. It was very short-sighted, but most people approach networking in this way, so I didn't think I was doing anything wrong.

networking events. On the rare occasion I attended these events, I didn't fully engage with the participants. I would look for obvious business connections where we could immediately help each other. It was very short-sighted, but most people approach networking in this way, so I didn't think I was doing anything wrong.

I decided to go to just a couple of these networking events consistently and really build some connections. When I did this, I found that I didn't need a lot of the content that I had developed and that the "fundamentals" were not that fundamental at all. Most of my sales are now face-to-face and come up during a normal conversation, no PowerPoint slides needed. One thing you will need is a good 20-30 second description of your business and what you're selling (sometimes called an elevator speech), but other than that my sales process is highly organic. It was difficult to give up my paperwork; slide decks are the crutch corporate America leans on. I didn't like it, but once I got used to it and had some success without the slide decks and formalities, it made my business a whole lot simpler.

What did you learn from the experience?

My experience taught me some things that I incorporate into my business every day. The first thing was that business relationships are made over time. I realized this during a networking event. Networking events are kind of funny to watch, especially the larger ones where people don't know each other at all. Many people who go to these events are looking for a quick sale and stop paying attention to someone once they decide that person can't help them immediately. Unsurprisingly, there aren't many success stories at these events because it's nearly impossible to build a relationship instantly. I've found that it's best to be patient. Don't try to find instant sales; try to find someone you can help or someone who you'll benefit from speaking to several times over the next month. It's a better way to build a relationship than trying to create one instantly, and it helps develop a mutual, genuine interest in each other's success.

Another thing that I've learned from networking is that

almost **ANYONE** *can be a good connection.*

You're not just building a relationship with the person; you're building an indirect relationship with their network. What I've noticed is that people tend to make snap decisions about a person when they first meet them, based mostly on how they can help them immediately. I admit, I used to do this too. Now when I network, I pay more attention to the type of person with whom I'm talking. Are they there just to take from me? Or, are they trying to build a network of people who they'll work with for the next ten years? When I network now I still size people up when I meet them, but now I think more about if a person "gets it" and is trying to build relationships. By doing this, I've surrounded myself with some great people and have built solid business relationships where everyone prospers.

Despite all the technology we have available to us, a referral is still the best way to generate business. Don't get me wrong, I'm a huge fan of technology and use it all the time in my business. However, there is no more likely sale than when a person comes to you through a referral. Referrals bring instant trust and credibility. You don't have to sell yourself as much as you would with someone you just met (whether that's in person or online). Referrals are all about relationships. If you develop good relationships with your colleagues and customers, then referrals can be a big part of your business model. I've had clients in the past who were frustrated by their sales process. The first thing I asked them was what percentage of their business came from referrals. If their answer was zero, then the first thing we discussed was how they're building relationships with their clients and colleagues. More often than not, this was not an area that they had spent a lot of time thinking about, and was typically an easy way to improve their business.

What did you learn about yourself from this experience?

I learned that I like the reason I created my business. There are a lot of reasons that people go into business, and at the end of the day we all worry about money, but I do what I do so that I can help people. I get to help my clients build and grow their businesses so that they can have the success of their dreams. I help my colleagues by referring people to them and using their services when I'm able. I feel I create a lot of good in the world and I'm more able to do this because of how I build relationships with my colleagues and clients.

I also learned that I enjoy my business more now that I build good relationships. When I started this business, I wasn't nearly as focused on relationships. I spent more time worrying about numbers and processes because that's what I did before I went into business for myself. It was very effective at the time and I was good at what I did, but when you run a small business you need something more. A small business needs a personality all its own. I started to build that once I stepped away from my computer and started making my business more about relationships. What I found was that I enjoy this part of the job. I like telling people about my business and learning about what other people do.

What do you believe are the most important characteristics and skills one must possess to have a successful life?

I think the most valuable characteristic anyone can have is persistence. I've rarely done anything exactly right the first time. Really, can anyone say they did something perfectly the first time? It almost never happens, so the only way for anyone to achieve their dreams is to

....

be PERSISTENT *and continue to work toward those dreams regardless of past failures.*

....

There are over seven billion people on the planet, and if you have a goal worth reaching you can bet there are plenty of others who want the same thing you do. You can't just try something for a week and then give up because there are too many other people out there who are trying to reach the same goal and are putting in more effort. Other variables may come into play, but if you're the person who is the most persistent in achieving a goal then that persistence is going to contribute to your success as much as anything else.

How do you use these skills and characteristics in your home, business and for your clients?

My new approach has improved my ability to serve my clients. I take care of my customers and want every project to end on a positive note so they'll come back to me for more coaching. I also help them apply this strategy to their businesses. Many business owners, especially online businesses, don't develop the relationships they need to grow their businesses the way they want. I coach them on how to build relationships and how not to ruin them once they are established.

I remember one client who was frustrated with his sales process. He felt it took up too much of his time, which kept him from doing his job. What I found was that almost all his business was from new customers. He had very little repeat business, almost no referrals, and had to start from square one with every sale. We worked through some of the reasons he wasn't getting repeat business and he began to build good relationships so that he did get repeat business and even some referrals. The funny part was that it really didn't have anything to do with his work. The issue was mostly how he managed his relationships with his clients. It was a huge help to this one client, just like it had been a huge help to me when I first started focusing on the relationship part of my business.

By: Erik Clark

Erik is an experienced management consultant with a track record of developing and implementing simple yet powerful business strategies to understand today's most critical business issues. Erik has worked with Fortune 500 companies across the globe and his insight has provided valuable strategic insight for retail, industry, private equity, and public-sector clients in the areas of business strategy, finance, operations strategy, and IT.

SURVIVING TO MOVE TOWARDS SOMETHING GREATER

By: Tina Byrd

For twenty years, I felt imprisoned and forced to fit the mold of the corporate world. I integrated into workplace culture, watched promotions happen by corporate politics and feared retaliation for my boldness. I was cornered into choosing between ethics or conforming to unfair corporate bias. By the end of the day, I was exhausted! The dreaded commute to work, the long corporate hours with no breaks and when I came home, I had to struggle to muster up the strength to give what little I had left to my family.

....

My life sucking J-O-B *or* *my* FAMILY *was often the* DILEMMA.
I WAS LOSING CONTROL
of my life and losing myself.

....

I couldn't remember the last time that I had said "yes" to family activities without feeling exhausted or having extreme feelings of guilt. It seemed the only thing that I had achieved was havoc! As for time for myself? Fuhgeddaboudit! To top it all off, the J-O-B wasn't even that fulfilling and didn't satisfy my God given purpose and passions, which brought even more guilt!

I worked so hard to obtain degrees and certifications, invested a lot of time into personal and professional development which catapulted me into being a successful, impactful and respected leader. I climbed up the corporate ladder, earned titles and a six-figure income and became very good at fitting into this type of environment. In today's economy, how many people would **LOVE** to be in my position?

But…why wasn't I more satisfied? Why did I feel so suffocated? Because I knew my calling was greater than any office titles, falsetto corporate success or compromised values of the all mighty fortune 500 company.

I remember so clearly feeling defeated! I brought my best game; my heart and creative soul, but my best was never going to be rewarded to my satisfaction. I was a butterfly trapped in a cage dying to break free to give the world all that I had within me!

I was so frustrated; I threw my hands up and made myself a priority. This is where I reflected on the relentless struggle and the countless sacrifices, I had made to make some other entity rich. Get a job, stay with that company, earn a paycheck, get benefits and retire. I mean, that is the J-O-B, right?

All of the sudden, I had an epiphany and my mindset shifted. Why make someone else rich? Why call someone else "Boss"? Why stay in this insidious black hole of frustration and anxiety? How did I expect things to change if I kept doing the same thing? Why should I accept not getting paid for the value, expertise, knowledge and other accolades I bring to a company?

Oh yeah….

....

It was **TIME** *to take control of my life,*

MAKE DIFFERENT DECISIONS AND CHOICES

so that I could finally live the life
I knew I was meant to live.

....

It was then, as the new claimed Boss of my life, that I made ONE of the biggest decisions! I **INTENTIONALLY BROKE FREE** from my life sucking J-O-B on MY terms! For the first time, I could see the light at the end of the funnel. It was dim, but it was there where it had not been before. I knew that life didn't have to be this way and that I could custom design the life I wanted. After all, I only have one life and no time to waste.

I anchored both feet into my faith. It's important to me that God always leads my direction and after lots of intense prayer and soul searching, I got the clarity, confirmation and direction for the next phase of my life. I knew exactly how I was supposed to be serving others and in what capacity.

I AM a Speaker/Coach/Consultant/Author/Personal and Professional Development Workshop Guru who has a passion to move others forward in life!

Working professionals/businesses hire me to defy the odds of **STAGNATION** to get **IMMEDIATE RESULTS** because most are lost, unfulfilled and frustrated so **I HELP** them refine and define success. Bottom line, they command the "now" to own their greatness!

How did I make this all happen?

I broke out the whiteboard and went to work to get crystal clear about the "what" and the "how".

I wanted to:

1) utilize my natural strengths, talents, skills, passions and knowledge to tap into my greatest potential

2) create a legacy of character, love and make positive impacts in people's lives

3) make a difference with helping people accomplish their dreams and goals

4) build healthy long-lasting relationships that are mutually beneficial

5) be in control of my surroundings and make my own schedule

6) be empowered and creative as I live each day in the moment

7) be fearless and fulfilled at the end of the day

8) be bold and unapologetically me

I didn't want to:

1)   be imprisoned in a cubicle/office or on conference calls all day

2)   choose between my family's activities or work demands

3)   work long hours for someone else with no reward

4)   be fearful and timid rather than bold and brave

5)   deal with bad bosses and double standards

6)   play in the sandbox with office politics

7)   compromise my ethics and values

8)   be unfulfilled and uninspired

Then, I created a two-year exit strategy with realistic timelines and leveraged my network. This was the **KEY STEP** in creating my survival plan because living without a constant paycheck is scary and stressful. Two years passed and I was fully operational and generating some cash flow into my bank account. It was time! Time to step out of my comfort zone and leave a world that I have known all my life, have been very successful in and reaped lots of benefits from. I dove headfirst into full time Multiprenuership!

Leaving corporate life sounds **AMAZING** but I'm not going to lie; it was very scary but exciting all at the same time. It's not for someone who is not willing to walk in **fear,** take **huge risks** or someone who is not **fully committed.** There are rough waters and storms throughout the process. The truth is, I work harder now than I ever did in corporate America. My days are longer not because I am not being efficient or effective, but because each day I continue to build **<u>MY</u> EMPIRE.** It's **ALL** worth it! It means something to me.

....

Lives are CHANGING
and I get to be part of that!

....

I say all of this because Entrepreneurship is not a destination, it is a journey. There will be hard knocks, times of joy and more than a few setbacks.

Through all this, I have learned to recognize my obstacles, align my thought process with my purpose and focus on what **I CAN** control. I have personally grown and been challenged exponentially to heights I never imagined. Every day, I'm blessed because NOW, **I AM** living my **BEST** life and making a difference in this world.

Our constitution only promises the **PURSUIT** of happiness, it does not promise happiness itself. None of us have a guarantee of success which is why life is a constant challenge every day and we **MUST** push past our **limited thinking** and **limited beliefs** to see what is possible!

By: Tina Byrd

Tina Byrd is a corporate America **SURVIVOR** who spent most of her career in leadership positions. She has given 20 years of her life as an unfulfilled employee, profiting someone else's company and wasting her talents with nothing to show for her passion except a monotonous, mundane existence. Observing her surroundings, she discovered that she was not alone. She witnessed how tired and disgruntled other's around her were as well; Vital, passionate people who longed to be awakened to their full potential, rather than be merely a number. At her wits end, she vowed to regain control of her life, conquered her fears, her doubts and intentionally transitioned into a successful Multipreneur.

Tina and her husband already established Classic Home Billiards (www.classichomebilliards.com) which is a full retail/service billiard business that focuses on bringing families together while having fun. However, that was just not fully satisfying her appetite to help people personally and professional so she created Coach Me, LLC (www.coachmellc.com). She designedly works with working professionals who are ready to explore and conquer the exciting world of Entrepreneurship and works with people who want or need to grow their careers and themselves. Her group work introduces her "Big three E's" (Experience, Expertise and Education) to get you to thrive in personal/professional growth, career transition and/or career advancement.

By: Tina Byrd

Working with Tina will identify barriers, remove fear and bring clarity and SOLUTIONS to issues. She also delivers clear guidance toward implementing efficient and effective personalized solutions and strategies to obtain reachable goals, results and prosperity.

Click here (or go to www.coachmellc.com Freebies Tab) for INSTANT access to YOUR tips to command the NOW and OWN your greatness!

Scan me

DOG IN A CRATE, A POLICE ESCORT, AND A TICKET ON FLIGHT #646

By: Cheryl Lynn Fields

It was a sunny afternoon in Savannah, GA when, at 2:15 on October 10, 2003 my phone rang. It was my two daughters, both emotional and trying to hold back the tears as they said to me "Mom, we love you so much and we can't bear to think of the rest of our lives without you. We know you're in an abusive relationship, and we want you to know that we are so scared for you. We want you back. So, we've booked a hotel room for you on the River Walk tonight, and a ticket on flight #646 leaving Savannah in the morning. We've arranged for a police escort just to be sure you make it on the flight. Will you be there? Please....please be there We want you to come home!" The flood of tears ran down my cheeks. I couldn't speak.

They were right.

....

For almost 2 YEARS
I had been in an ABUSIVE RELATIONSHIP, and I truly was in DANGER.

....

I thought I'd been hiding it. I thought that, somehow, I could "fix" it and everything would be OK.

But, my daughters, in their mid-twenties at the time, could see the pain, shame, and heartache that consumed me every minute of every day. They were offering me a way out….and I knew I had to take it. If not, how could I ever look them in the eyes again…or worse. Maybe I wouldn't even be here to have that option.

I'd always been so strong; building businesses, as a single mom, from Hollywood, CA to Grand Junction, Co and then an international business journal that was distributed to Maine and Atlantic Canada. Bootstrapping every step of the way. Every venture was an adventure that we tackled together. We had (still have) an amazing relationship and an unbreakable bond.

But now I was the one needing help, needing support, strength and guidance from the only souls that mattered to me…and they were all I had. I was about to make one of the biggest decisions in my life and there was no time to waste. I had to act swiftly while I still could. I wanted to throw up.

I gathered many of the items that were most important to me from his house where I was living, tucked pictures in my oversized bag, and packed clothes into the largest suitcase I could find. I was shaking as I headed for the door – knowing I needed to be long gone by the time he got back…or who knows what wrath I would face. Exactly the confrontation I wanted to avoid.

I walked out. My dog, Durango, on a leash, suitcase on rollers, and overstuffed bag over my shoulder, I walked out the front door as if it was just another day in my life.

··

"Pull yourself together"
I kept REPEATING *in* MY MIND,
but it wasn't that easy.

··

Or was it?

When I met him I had a business, a home, and a car that I loved. In the 2 years we were together, he convinced me that he wanted "better" things for us to share in "the good life". So he bought me a new BMW sports car, asked me to live with him in the beautiful home we picked out together in Savannah GA, and helped me sell my business so that we were free to travel and enjoy life.

Instead, in retrospect, I realize that it was his way of having complete control – as now the car was no longer in my name, or the house, or even the business for that matter. I was stuck.

As I walked in the direction of the hotel, I passed Forsythe Park and the beautiful fountain that is so famously pictured in anything about Savannah. As I sat down on a bench near the fountain, I realized that it was, in fact, the exact bench that Tom Hanks sat on when they filmed the movie Forrest Gump. And where he famously said "Life's like a box of chocolates. You never know what you're going to get". No one knew that better than I did at that moment.

I sat on the bench and thought about my life.

How did I get here? And why? How could I let this happen? As I thought about all that had gone wrong for me in my life, I felt myself sinking deeper and deeper into the depression of my past and a numbness came over me like a crashing wave.

I thought how wonderful to live a life of simplicity, happiness, and wonder. I wanted to go back to who I was before. I wondered if I could find that again. Only time would tell.

Today was a pivot. And things were about to change. And change they did.

It started with a decision.

I thought about my girls, and how much I loved them. How much it meant that they were taking charge of a situation that I had let get way out of hand. That they saw through me, and my situation, and loved me anyway. They realized I made a mistake and they were standing with me hand in hand to get my life back on track.

I started thinking about my daughters getting married and having kids. How wonderful it would be to have a growing family and children who would be our family's next generation. How would I want to be known or remembered? What type of person would I have to be to be proud and confidant again? How could I take this experience and use it for my own good? These questions were getting harder to answer, so I went back to the thought of grandkids. How wonderful that would be? But WAIT…

What if my daughters (who weren't even dating anyone serious at the time – so why grandkids were my priority I have no idea. What I was going to have for dinner seems like a much more pressing issue!) each married someone and moved away, how would I be able to see them? How could I travel? All sorts of emotions came rushing in.

The thought of that was frightening. I felt sick again.

I realized that I needed to make a big change in my life. I needed to change the way that I was thinking about my life. I knew I needed to make a lifechanging decision.

And that I did.

....

I REALIZED *I knew how* BUSINESS *worked,* but *I didn't know how* MONEY *worked.*

....

I thought that financial advisers always seemed to drive nice cars, have nice homes and enjoy their time on the golf course. They surely must know how money works, so I decided to become a financial adviser. I spent thousands of dollars on education, passed my tests, and was hired by a global investment firm right out of school.

I was new in the industry early in 2008, and we all know what happened later that year…The CRASH! The economy crashed, the real estate market crashed, and the stock market crashed. People were in a state of panic. I saw other advisers telling their clients they had lost 20, 30 or 40% of all they had worked so hard all their lives to save. I heard them saying "don't buy that vacation home, don't quit your job, and don't purchase that trip you planned for you and your spouse. Retirement is not an option for you now." How could this be?

As they were trying to stop the losses in their client's accounts, advisers were racking up more and more fees, causing the account values to drop even further. More trading, more fees. Less money in the account. The cycle seemed never ending.

I went home every night, feeling that NOW I had made another really big mistake in my life. Besides all the time and expense, I was now certified in a system that I didn't believe in. A system that had failed so many great Americans and their families and, yes, a system that had failed me and my family as well.

As I laid my head on the pillow one night, I wondered "what do wealthy people do? Because they don't start over every time the stock market crashes, and they always have time *and* money. And not only enough money for *their* lives, but enough left over to *pass* on to the next generation." So why wasn't I taught this in financial adviser school?

I woke up the next morning with a new plan of action rolling around and around in my thoughts. So I did what Napoleon Hill did in "Think and Grow Rich" and I started interviewing wealthy people to find out what was working for them, and how I could tap into the same strategies for myself, and for my clients in the future.

What I found is that there's a system for those who aren't willing to pay tax over and over on the same money; a way, using the IRS tax code, that you can pay tax only once on the money, and then let it grow for you tax free for the rest of your life! This is how the wealthy did it (think Rockefellers, Walt Disney, Ray Croc of McDonalds, The Pampered Chef, and J.C. Penny) And I realized that it was available to anyone and everyone! I knew I had found my life's work, and I was so excited to become an expert in the strategies.

Fast forward, I now speak across the country to associations, business groups and women's groups about how you can increase the cash flow in your business, up level your lifestyle, have tax free income in retirement that will last your entire life, and then leave a legacy for those you love or causes you care about. I wanted to shout it from every rooftop I could find!

For the last decade, I've enjoyed the freedom I could only imagine back in 2003 as I sat on that park bench. I am loving my life and love the people I've been able to help get free from financial worry, while creating a rock solid financial foundation for themselves and their families so that they can go out into the world and contribute; to be all that they are destined to be and to be able to fulfill their life's purpose.

As I look back on that fateful day in October of 2003, I can hardly even remember what it felt like to be lost, alone, scared and broke.

I was dependent on someone at the expense of my wellbeing, and those days are long gone. I let someone else be my source of financial stability, and I will never make that mistake again. I will never give away the power that is my God-given right, and I'll live my life to the fullest knowing I have a rock-solid financial foundation that will never lose value.

There is so much to love about life, and about the intrinsic value that we possess as humans living out our life on this planet. We are destined for greatness, and it is ours for the taking.

As I look back at my fears on that park bench (not being able to travel to see my kids and grandkids) it's so easy for me to see that all of that was necessary for me to emerge as the person I am today.

I was living in Charleston, SC when my oldest daughter got married and pregnant later that year. She and her husband were living in south Florida and I came to visit 4 days each month for almost 4 years. I was not going to miss any of the joy, anticipation, and the excitement of my first granddaughter coming into this world and being there for her first words, her first steps, and her first birthday! There are now 4 precious little souls that I get to spend time with, explore life with, and be the "Mimi" that they look up to and share life's' experiences with.

As I made each of the 48 trips to visit them, I remembered to feel the gratitude that my new life had afforded me: the ability to visit whenever I wanted, JUST BECAUSE I COULD.

Now I'm remarried, and my husband and I live just a few miles away from them.

It's the **LIFE** *I've* **DESIGNED** *for* **MYSELF** *and a* **LIFE** *I love.*

I take Wednesday afternoons off to help with homework, ride bikes, play with the horses, or just have conversations about whatever is bubbling up for them in their young lives.

I've realized that even in the "park bench" moments, life is always working for us. All we have to do is have the courage to ask the right questions and allow the answers to challenge us to be the best we can be. We have to have faith. We have to have the courage to make a decision.

It's all there for each one of us. We just have to make a decision to go get it.

By: Cheryl Lynn Fields

After having to start over in life at 47, I knew my life needed drastic changes in several areas. I decided to go back to school and studied to be a financial planner. I completed my studies, became licensed just in time for the market to crash in 2008.

I, along with everyone else, lost much of what I had worked so hard to save.

As I heard my colleagues in the other cubicles telling people "you can't retire," and "don't quit your job," and worse of all "you've lost 20 or 30 or 40% of all of your life savings," I felt disheartened. In all honesty, it made me sick to my stomach, and I realized that I was in an industry that made absolutely no sense.

How can we believe in a system that lets people lose everything they've worked all their lives for - gone virtually overnight?

This burning question fueled curiosity in me, to where I now was asking, "what do wealthy people do?" Because...

1) They don't start over every time the stock market crashes

2) They always have time AND money

3) They have enough money for their lives and their next generations lives as well.

I decided to interview wealthy people to find out what exactly it was that they were doing that the rest of us weren't taught. Here's what I discovered.

By: Cheryl Lynn Fields

There are two systems:

1) One is for people that want to pay tax over and over again on the same money.

2) And the other system is for people who want to pay tax only once on the money they earn.

Which would you choose?

I show people how to increase the cash flow in their business, up level their lifestyle by getting out of debt, have tax-free income in retirement, and leave a legacy for those they love and causes they care about.

Want to know more? Scan below to get your complimentary 3-part video series telling you about the EASY or the HARD WAY when it comes to your finances!

Scan me

THANK YOU FOR STEALING MY INVENTION!

By: Nancy White

The one defining moment that changed the trajectory of my entrepreneurial journey was when someone I trusted stole my invention. But first, let me paint the picture for you, by rewinding just a little bit.

After leaving corporate America to become a stay at home Mom and an aspiring entrepreneur,

··

I DISCOVERED *I had* NO IDEA
what being an ENTREPRENEUR *entailed.*

··

In hindsight, I'm not surprised because my life followed a typical formula: grow up, it is no wonder that I was taken unawares. After all, I had grown up, gone to school, and entered the workforce. I had four different corporate jobs - all four situations where my boss telling me what to do and what not to do. It wasn't until I became a Mother, a role which I lovingly refer to as a Pro-bono Home Making Engineer, that I took the into the vast unknown- an entrepreneurial adventure that has lasted 36 years and counting.

To kickstart my new work-for-myself life, I did what I do best – research! My previous job had been as a nation-wide researcher in Human Resources for the local government. I knew how to dig in and find just about anything.

These were the days long before Google, emails and the Internet. Instead, we rummaged through libraries to hunt down information and chased important documents and prized pieces of information via snail mail. Yes that meant sending forms back and forth to agencies and companies using envelopes and stamps. Why was I doing this? Because I had an idea for an invention! And though I knew my goal was for my first invention, the 'how to' was still to be determined. So, reverse engineering made sense to me, plus I was determined to learn as I proceeded. My motto was to "Get 'er done". I knew I had a great idea and I was determined to see it come to fruition! And it did, but not with me as the licensed creator! Can you say devastation!?!.

This was 1986, after conducting a nation-wide survey by mail to determine interest in my invention, I hired an artist to draw up specs, research trademark availability, and registered for a trademark. I also hired an attorney, to make sure all my paperwork was in order, and to start the painstaking process of sending and receiving non-compete confidentiality agreements. Finally, we got all the paperwork in place, and I was ready to sell my invention idea to a manufacturer! After many, many attempts and rejections, there was one company extremely interested. We exchanged several letters and long-distance calls. I WAS SO EXCITED!

Then silence.

Not a peep from the company, and my attorney was having no luck getting them to respond.

Then, a year later, I saw my invention come to fruition with the very company that said they were interested. But it didn't have my name on it! Instead, I believe my dishonest attorney, whom I paid and had put my trust in, had not protected me. I was not in a position for a long, drawn out legal battle with a corporation with deep pockets. I felt shocked and betrayed!! How? Why? The questions kept coming. Then I realized that my determination, "get 'er done" doggedness and my Lone Ranger approach had instead "done her in". After considering a few courses of action, I eventually closed that door. Disappointed, rejected and tainted from the whole experience, I gave my entrepreneurial quest a rest for a short time. I am sure a lot of you have experienced similar circumstances, and you just had to get back on the horse to ride again. After all that is a major characteristic of an entrepreneur isn't it? There have been many who gave up all hope for success - too rejected to go on, but not me. Thankfully, hopes and dreams were born again in this entrepreneur's mind and heart. I moved forward; a whole lot wiser. This is how it happened.

More Lone Ranger: Remember I had forged ahead thinking I had all the answers? I had gone it alone (aside from my dishonest attorney). Looking back, it would have been much smarter to have found someone who had successfully brought their invention to market and asked for their guidance.

Not ASKING for help, TAUGHT me a GREAT LESSON that PROPELLED me into a renewed DETERMINATION to create SUCCESS.

This time I put my efforts in proper order. I prayed first. Next I asked for help in the planning, brainstorming process, and received valuable feedback from some retired business professionals with SCORE. It was an amazing time of evaluation and creation. - one that I had never imagined possible. It was a time when my prayers, energy and hopes were renewed. To this day, I still utilize the awesome organization SCORE. They have evolved with technology and expanded their offerings to many businesses and hopeful entrepreneurs.

Determination: Yes - there was a thought or two about returning to Corporate America. But I truly trusted and believed the best was yet to come and, with sheer determination, I forged ahead.

Having been knocked down, but refusing to give up, also revealed my resiliency to myself and others. Some people would call not giving up stubbornness, I call it my tenacious spirit!

Growing from Lessons Learned: I had a lot going for me but needed to know more about starting and running a business. Just inventing something does not create a business. I also learned that even if you have a signed letter of confidentiality, you need unlimited resources if you're going to legally fight a large company. An entrepreneur must not dwell in the past but must learn

learn from the past and keep on going. The beauty of entrepreneurs is that we discover a need or a want and provide a solution. We also have to support and collaborate with others utilizing each other's gifts, talents and resources to be successful. These are key lessons that are at the core of my journey, even today.

Integrity: Doing the right thing, even when others don't see it, is an important characteristic in and out of business. Being honest or dishonest is attached to the law of sowing and reaping. You have to choose. Sooner or later what you sow comes to harvest.

Never Stop Learning & Growing: Lifelong learning is essential and a choice. The process is unique for everyone. Discover how you learn best and then keep on keeping on. It is the key to growing, evolving your business and staying relevant.

Embrace the Tech: Embracing technology is a snap for some and a stumbling block for others. If you want your business to grow and thrive, either you or someone trustworthy must incorporate technology to help run your business.

Know Your Stuff: Be informed about every system, every process, and every procedure of your business. Know where every contact is that supports the mechanics of your operations. Think of it this way: if you are thinking about selling your business or if you are unable to run your business, could someone else take over? Being organized and having systems in place can save a lot of time, money and stressful moments.

Use What You've Got: I believe that to be successful in business and life, you have to use your gifts, talents, and skills to enhance the lives of others. That belief has especially guided my entrepreneurial journey. A daily goal for me is to have peace and contentment at the end of each day. Peace is a result of my efforts to take care of what has been entrusted to me, starting with myself and extending to my personal and professional relationships. Gifts and talents require nurturing, and it is important to fine tune our skills.

Networking 2.0: Speaking of skills, it is a skill to talk with people, but a gift to listen and truly learn what is in their best interest. It is a skill to network on and offline but a talent to guide people into potential collaborations or new resources. It is a skill to know how to strategize and market and a talent to bring your vision to fruition. We need it all working together, all of our gifts, talents and skills.

Personally, using my skills, gifts and talents wrapped up in my character is always an adventure and mostly a fun one! My clients know that they are the priority of our conversations and times together. Being yourself, honoring others, and being respectful goes a long way in business and life.

Grace and Space: Over the years I have learned to value a permission-based approach when sharing information with others or offering my '2 cents'. "May I make a suggestion?" is received a lot better than, "Let me tell you what I think." I give a lot of grace and space to people, whether they deserve it or not. We never know what is going on in people's lives. When we allow our thoughts and imaginations to create a reason or story about what we can rightly never know, we just fueled our stress levels. Don't get me wrong, I can bless and release in a nanosecond if someone does not do what they say when they say they are going to do something. But remember, we get to pick and choose what we attach our emotions to, and we get to be responsible for our own choices and actions. When I mess up I own it, apologize and do my best to correct the situation.

Give Yourself a Hand: I also celebrate victories, small and big. I clap a lot! The majority of people don't stop to celebrate their accomplishments and are off and running to conquer the next task. I've learned to savor every small victory as each small victory builds the foundation of success.

Since my entrepreneur journey began, I have started several businesses. Some failed like the first one, some flopped and some succeeded! Currently, I have been building and operating my Health and Wellness business for the last 12 years, along with side stream incomes - we all need multiple resources in this day and time. Even at the beginning of my current business, I had a learning experience. I laughed at myself when I thought it would be an oxymoron to wreck my health building my Health and Wellness business. I will always be a lifelong learner and proactively manage stress so stress does not manage me!

Being an **ENTREPRENEUR** *and operating a* **BUSINESS** *has unlimited* **TWISTS** *and* **TURNS.**

Having great support systems, a solid foundation, ongoing reviews/updates, unlimited intellectual resources, and a network of people to both cheer you on and provide valuable input is paramount. And never be too proud to "Ask for more Help and Accept It". I wish you great success in your entrepreneurial lifestyle and the satisfaction of using your gifts, talents and skills to enhance the lives you touch. I learned on a deeper level how much I want to make sure that every action I take makes the lives of other people better. This is the best lesson I could have ever received.

Nancy White wants to live in a world where people will thrive and not just survive both physically and financially. Her business is to assist health conscious adults in creating their healthy lifestyles they can tweak as they age.

Her quest to live a preventative, healthy lifestyle began with the premature deaths of her father and brother from cancer. Her mother lived to 96 without any major illness and was a great influence for incorporating natural healthy solutions and natural remedies.

Nancy started her entrepreneurial journey 35 years ago after leaving corporate America. Since that time she has started several businesses, some flopped, some sold, some blossomed, but learning has never stopped.

A natural gift for Nancy is connecting people, especially for business. She has served as the Foundation leader for eWomen Network since 2006, established the first Heart Link Network for women in Charlotte in 2008 and is part of other chambers and networking groups. She was once referred to as the "most connected person" in Charlotte.

By: Nancy White

Nancy loves speaking to women's groups with her fun stop sign. Her first book, The G.R.T. Journal is an Amazon Best Seller and there is a second book to hit the shelves in the Fall of 2019. Nancy is one of the Hosts & Executive Producers of The Network Show, to be launched August 2019. She has been cultivating her Healthy Cells Chick business since 2007, which at the end of the day is her heart throb making a difference in assisting people in creating their healthy lifestyles.

Please connect with me to talk about your healthy lifestyle endeavors and receive your FREE healthy wheel assessment with healthy suggestions.

Just released! G.R.T. Journal, Gratitude, Reflections and Tips. A personal tool to help you achieve your goals. Sold on Amazon

Ways for us to stay in touch -

Facebook - The Healthy Cells Chick
Linkedin - NancyWhiteTheHealthyCellsChick
Instagram - HealthyCellsChick
Email - info@thehealthycellschick.com
Phone - 704.756.9295

Scan me

LIGHT AT THE END OF THE PODCAST FUNNEL

By: Brenda Pearce

As a high school student, I loved school. So much so that my senior year came and almost passed before I decided my future career path. It was at deadline time that I decided to go into nursing. It is truly surprising that I made that choice as everyone knew of my fear of blood. It surprises me to this day that I made that choice. I guess I felt that I was facing my fear. A dare to myself, to face what feared me.

So I selected one school, one campus and one program. I had no fear of not being selected. I was resolved and determined, and despite my fears, felt unflappable. Sure enough, after the interviews, and, the admission process, I was selected. I share this because looking back, this was such a feat of manifestation. When you know that you know...

On the first day of training, all those years ago, the first exercise was to look to the left and to the right, and then told to remember those faces, as half of them will be gone by Christmas. Wow. As a high school overachiever, this was not going to happen to me. The gauntlet was cast, and determination kicked in. Having never failed or quit anything in my life,

I was **DETERMINED** *to* **SUCCEED** *despite*
my **FEARS** *and* **INHIBITIONS.**

Yes, by Christmas, just a little less than half the class remained. I was still standing!

As the program advanced onto second year, the training and experiences intensified. It was a continued shock and awe as we moved into more confidence. Immersion into all aspects of nursing often put us into the front row of procedures. Draped in isolation gowns, surgical masks and packed closely in warm and small spaces, I would hold my breath as I fixated on what was going on in front of me. I was often found passed out cold on the floor. This happened frequently.

I was summoned to the office of the Program Director and asked to consider my career objectives. I remember politely acknowledging her concerns and expressing my determination to continue and complete the program. Onwards!

So even though I continued to periodically pass out, I did make it! I graduated and passed all of the exams and became a RN. Hard to believe, that it has been over 35 years since those first tentative years. I have always known, in my heart, that in the diverse world of healthcare and nursing, I would find my niche. And… yes there have been further incidences in which I have passed out or felt queasy.

Through the years, and the various settings that I have practiced in, I have learned a lot about life. I have learned ever so much more from caring for the dying. It opens up a whole new perspective of what life is all about. It has empowered and inspired me and helped me to realize what it truly means to be alive. I thank those who have taught me that life is not a dress rehearsal, and that we all should lighten up. Laugh more and smile often.

It was particularly important to embrace these lessons when going through my own personal trials and tribulations.

It was during my years as a mom to my younger children, when I was dealing with parenthood, work-life and trying to be mom and dad that I hit my wall. My husband was often away from home as a truck driver, and I was totally drained. I was giving too much of myself to everyone and everything, and I was stretched too thin. It was at that time, as an answer to prayer, that I found inspiration online through teleseminars. Hearing the words of Wayne Dyer, Louise Hay, Abraham-Hicks and others of the transformational world,

I found peace, and new thoughts. It was my therapy and my heart was filled with hope, inspiration and empowerment. I listened avidly after the kids were in bed.

Fast forward through the next several years; the kids grew, and divorce happened. Free at last to determine my future life, a new frontier presented itself. An opportunity to learn how to create and host my own teleseminar series fell into my lap. I took advantage of the opportunity and hence, the Healthy Wealthy Evolution was born. Having NO technical skills, but determination to succeed, I learned how to connect with some of the inspired teachers that had helped to heal me. I learned how to develop a virtual following and was thrilled that people would care to listen to me from all over the world.

I soon realized that what I was doing was similar to a radio talk show. It was the very early days of podcasting, and I actually felt that I was doing 'Internet Radio'. My final season ended up being a 60-speaker event. Originally meant to be a 20 speaker event, I just kept adding new speakers to the series and was looking to see how I could do internet radio.

Again,

MANIFESTATION *led me to* CONNECT *with* SOMEONE *who could get me* *onto a* PODCAST NETWORK,

and I started as a host. Again, determination and experience helped me to overcome my trepidation in this new realm. Armed with learned skills from my summit series, and marketing skills that I embraced, and the determination of a nurse, I found my new love… Podcasting.

Through my 6 years of podcasting, I have honed my identity as The Empowered Nurse. I triage body-mind-spirit and combine my love of empowerment, inspiration, wellness and well-being. I have learned to use my podcast to elevate guests, provide great content and inspire listeners. Reaching a global audience is amazing as well. Reaching potential clients makes podcasting a readily available go to in today's global marketplace.

PODCASTING *sets you* APART *in the* WORLD.

It creates a credibility that makes it possible to get your message across many different platforms and social media. It is an amazing media that transcends borders and boundaries. It has a global reach. It is something that you can add to your blogs. You can upload your podcasts onto YouTube. You can take the conversations and change them into transcripts. It is an unregulated broadcast platform. It can touch and change lives.

For this very reluctant nurse, to have achieved success through podcasting is such a thrill which has put into action my love of creativity and has helped me find my voice. It has helped me to move from behind the scenes to in front of the camera, as I produce and host my own local TV Show. I have also proved to this little-nurse-that-could, that I can do anything.

Over the last few years I have also helped several people to start their own podcasts. It has been a labor of love and has been done on a one-on-one basis. Again, using my creativity and my love of sharing the voices and stories that we all have, I am now stepping out to help more people discover and create podcasts. I am creating a comprehensive online program that will help more people glean from my own experiences, tips and secrets on how to create very professional and polished podcasts. My program helps with creating confidence and how to create graphics, intros, outros and how to syndicate their shows, create a marketplace and monetize their shows.

I feel that we all have a place in the cosmic conversation. Whether it is a talk or interview show, sharing a love of a hobby, sharing your music or humor, expertise as a coach or author, there is magic in creating media that matters.

I invite you, if you have a mission or message to share with the world, to connect with me. Glean from my years of experience and take this opportunity to make podcasting part of your global reach. Podcasting can be the light at the end of your funnel.

By: Brenda Pearce

Brenda Pearce is known as the "Empowered Nurse". She is an RN with a purpose and a message. She triages body-mind-spirit through your podcasts and is a Producer/Host of her own TV Show on the Rogers TV Network in Canada. She has appeared as a published best-selling contributing author in several books. She continues to work as a part time RN. Brenda has combined her love of wellness and well-being and is an integrative energy practitioner. She is readily accessible to help connect and coach you to achieve your podcast goals as part of your success funnel.

Visit: http://bit.ly/33ma1gP to connect further with Brenda, her work, and podcast coaching

FREE Gift: http://bit.ly/2SdT2a8

Scan me

GO WITHIN AND LISTEN TO YOUR ANSWERS

By: Erin Newman

What is the one defining moment during your entrepreneurial journey that transformed and changed the trajectory of your life and/or business?

I was sitting in the bathtub, crying to my husband, saying "I can't do this anymore. It's just too hard." I had invested in a big-time coach and was tired of feeling like a failure in my business and was ready to give it all up and throw the entire business in the metaphorical trashcan.

He patted my arm and said, "It's okay." (Maybe not the best consoling ever from a husband.)

But when he asked me if I wanted to go back to corporate, if I wanted "a real job" again, I already knew the answer:

....

for me, there has **NEVER** *been an* **OPTION** *to "go back".*

....

Because my work isn't about me or my small fears. (P.s. what does "real job" even mean?!)

My work is about changing lives, helping people to really follow their unique path, and not to listen to anyone else about their soul's work – that's the work that I do. It's only when I forget what I'm here for and instead focus on the income and the strategies and the numbers…that's when the #$%* hits the fan and I start to drown in all of those "real world" concerns.

Each time I go through one of those down moments, I return, again and again, to the work I teach my clients:

go within, ask for a DEEPER CONNECTION *to* SOURCE/UNIVERSE/GOD,

and listen to my answers. I ask "how can this be easier? Lighter? More fun?" And then I do what's being asked. That's the work.

How did you persevere during this moment?

In that moment in the bathtub, one of my biggest fears was that I wouldn't be able to pay off the bigtime coach. So I asked myself "Is this my heart or my head talking?" When I remember that I (we) always have divine support, in each and every moment, and that if my heart is saying "YES", that the universe will find a way to bring in that money…then I know that it's the right decision.

What did you learn from the experience?

It's a continual relearning. Pretending that we learn something one time and then we're done – well, it's not what actually happens. We have to keep learning it, over and over.

What did you learn about yourself from this experience?

I am continually learning that the universe is unlimited, that

ABUNDANCE *is* UNLIMITED, *and that I don't need to ever* PLACE *limits on what is possible for me.*

Or for my clients, either. My work is in seeing them as their best possible selves at all times and being able to help them to experience that.

What do you believe are the most important characteristics and skills one must possess to have a successful life?

A belief in one's self. The ability to follow your own path, even when everyone else is telling you to something else or to manage your business in a different way.

How do you use these skills and characteristics in your home business and for your clients?

I really free myself from having to stay within a narrow box of what it means to be a business coach. Yes, I teach business, but I teach it from the perspective of "what would be SUPER exciting for you to share? And what would be a SUPER exciting way to share it?" And then we work on the mindset that stops us from sharing what we really want to share, as well as the manifesting tools that we need to be utilizing in order to bring this big thing into existence.

By: Erin Newman

Erin Newman is an Authentic Courage Coach and Shamanic Mentor for smart, spiritual entrepreneurs. She helps business owners to bust through their subconscious blocks and fears in order to claim their magic and create a successful business on their terms.

Let's connect!

Website:
http://www.erinnewman.com/

Facebook:https://www.facebook.com/ErinNewmanMindsetCoach/

Linkedin: https://www.linkedin.com/in/erin-newmanlifecoach/

Special Gift for you! Scan the QR code to get my ebook: The Authentic Courage Guide: A Proven 3-Step Method to Uplevel Your Confidence and Create an Aligned, Authentic, and Successful Biz.

Scan me

CHAPTER 8: LIVING A ROYAL LIFE

By: Patti Phillips

Life had been a struggle for me the whole time I was married to my last husband. I won't share the term I usually refer to him by, but let's just say, he had a way of constantly turning our finances into a whirling cesspool! It didn't matter how hard and long we worked or how much money we made, we were constantly short on the bills, had a bill collector on the phone or at the door, or had "final notices" piled up in our mailbox.

....

I kept **THINKING** *that*
if I only **WORKED HARDER,**
we would **CATCH UP.**

....

If I only knew the right marketing plan to bring in more clients, I could make enough to get "caught up." At one point I worked 16- and 18-hour days for over 100 days straight, without a break. There was no time or money to enjoy my kids or my life. No time for fun and friendship. No money for the "extras" in life, all due to his lack of ability to be responsible financially. Finally, the realization hit me that until I left this marriage, this would be my story for the rest of my life. He helped cement my decision when my step-daughter caught him flirting on the phone with another woman. It wasn't his first "indiscretion" by any means. That was the impetus it took for me to call it "game over" and leave the marriage.

This was 2008 and I was a real estate agent. Due to the economy it was also about the worst time possible to be in my line of work. I was scared to death. My credit had been obliterated thanks to him and was in the low 400's. I had not only myself, but my kids to think about. My son was already on his own, but I had one daughter in college, and my 14-year-old stepdaughter was coming to live with me in my new home. I wasn't sure HOW I would manage – but I knew I had to make some drastic changes.

That's when I decided that I would **NEVER again** live my life like this. I would never simply live in "survival mode" working morning to night. Never again would I put myself in the position of letting a man run and ruin my finances. It was time that I took my life by the reigns and made it a life worth living. I knew only too well that we can't count on tomorrow. I have already outlived my mother by almost 10 years. The life I had been living was wasting precious time in the very short years we are given. My mom had a lot of regrets for the unfulfilled dreams in her life, which helped me to realize that tomorrow isn't promised, and life is far too short. It was time to get on to the life I deserved! A life of abundance and joy, fun and friendships, travel and adventure. And that's what happened!

I won't lie and say that it happened overnight, but the changes started immediately! I had always wanted to dance, and this was a perfect time to learn, so I called a client of mine who was a dancer and asked him where I could go to start learning. I started dancing, first one night a week, then two, then even more. Dancing became my "drug of choice" through the difficult time of rebuilding my life, my finances, and my career. The only thing I could focus on when dancing was what the next step was. That became my metaphor for life! It made me happy. I lost weight. I felt good about myself and I made new and wonderful friends.

I began to venture out from real estate to work on some "side gigs." As I did that I found that I became even more confident.

Making **MONEY** *came much easier than it had in* **YEARS.**

By: Patti Phillips

I started selling a line of cosmetics and health products, and through that company I earned some free trips and found that I made even more friends who were confident and successful in their lives.

One dream I had for years was to try performing stand-up comedy. Soon after my break-up, I did an open mic night and **LOVED** it. I did a few performances at that same comedy club, and then began dreaming of doing my own "one woman show." Before I knew it, the opportunity was presented to me, and I now perform regularly! I'm known as *The Comedy Queen*. There is a following of people who love my comedy, so when I put on a show; the room is typically full. When I am in front of the room performing, I have so much fun!

I love to have people in my home, and I love any excuse for a party. As my new life grew and developed, I started to frequently entertain at my home.

It seemed that the more fun I had, coincidentally, the more money I was making! Soon, travel, parties, dancing, dating, and new friends were a part of my day-to-day life. And my paycheck was supporting my life! There was just one problem: real estate was not "fun" for me. There was far too much stress and drama. Not to mention, when you are traveling, dealing with the stresses that can happen in real estate is draining. My "job" was cutting into my fun new life!

About the time that I was trying to figure out how to step back a bit from real estate more and into other venues, a young assistant I had hired said to me, "I'm SO impressed with you! You do so many things! You know how to throw great parties, you are organized, and you have an amazing life! You decide to do something, and WHAM, you are doing it, and excelling! You are like '*The Queen of Damn Near Everything!'* You should write a blog!"

So I did! I started a lifestyle blog, called--- funny enough, The Queen of Damn Near Everything. I have had my blog for a few years now and love sharing some of the fun in my life, whether it's something that tickles my funny bone, tips on entertaining, a rant that I just have to get off my chest, or some of our travel adventures… Whatever strikes my fancy, that's what goes into the blog.

I have coined a phrase that I now use very often, regarding living your best life. I call it "Living a Royal Life."

....

I truly BELIEVE *that each one of us* *can* BUILD A LIFE *that is* ENJOYABLE, HAPPY, *and full of* ADVENTURE.

....

Whatever it is that can make you feel that you are living the best life for *YOU.* After all, no one does *YOU* as well as you!

Many women put their family, their homes, their careers, caring for their parents---- EVERYTHING first before they think about themselves, their needs, their dreams, and their wants. They are in the same position I was, surviving, but not THRIVING. They are definitely not "Living a Royal Life." In fact, their lives are more like those of servants in the castle than the royalty!

A big part of my focus now is on helping women to live bigger, bolder lives filled with fun and adventure. I help them to figure out how to build their "Royal Life." Sometimes women are so overwhelmed they don't know where to begin.

You may not be able to completely walk away from the life you have, but you can change it one step at a time, one day at a time, one habit at a time. You need to figure out what works for you, make a list of what is important to you, then figure out what it takes to get there.

I often have people tell me that they see what I am doing, and how happy I am, and that I am "so lucky." I beg to differ. Where I am and the life I am living isn't due to luck. It's due to me deciding what I was going to accept for my life, who I was going to allow into my life, and what my perfect life looked like. Then, I took the steps I needed to weed out what wasn't working for me.

My life is lived full throttle. I no longer care what people think of me. I'm too outrageous for some. I know my lifestyle is far too hectic for many. They wouldn't want to fit into a day, a week, or a month what I do. I cram every bit of fun and adventure into my life that I possibly can, and I wouldn't have it any other way. You never know when they are going to "call in your chips"- and I don't ever want to look back and say I wish I had done something, gone somewhere, or experienced something that I haven't gotten to do! I'll never be finished, because there is far too much to do in life and the world is way too big to see it all. But I can be satisfied in the fact that I have done as much as possible the past 10 years since I turned my life around and began "Living a Royal Life."

Now I am having fun helping other women who just don't know where to begin map out their perfect life. It's always exciting to see what is important in someone else's life and plan. Sometimes all they need is to know that someone else has done it to succeeded!

Do you feel that you are "Living a Royal Life," your very best possible life? If not, have you considered that it might be time for a change? Have you dreamed about a different, more fulfilling, more fun-filled and abundant life, but thought that maybe it just wasn't in the cards for you? I believe that it IS possible for you to achieve a fabulous life. The problem is, YOU need to believe it, and then take the necessary steps to make it happen! I think you are worth it, do you? If you do, today can be the very first day toward "Living a Royal Life!"

Free Offer: Email Patti (Patti.Phillips57@gmail.com) to receive your list of 10 Steps to Living a Royal Life, and her free sticker, "Living A Royal Life!" Patti will be holding a contest for people sharing their sticker in different settings that show them living their best life!

By: Patti Phillips

Patti Phillips has been a resident of the San Diego area for 40 years, is the mom of 3 adult children, 2 whom she birthed, and one she acquired through other means. Known as "The Queen of Damn Near Everything", Patti wears many diverse, fun and creative hats. She is an author, artist, comedian, Realtor, speaker, serial entrepreneur, wedding officiant and blogger. Living her best life, with integrity, to the fullest while experiencing the most fun possible is Patti's passion! She feels that many women put themselves, their needs, their dreams and their goals last- and

she is out to change that by teaching others how to "Live a Royal Life."

Scan me

DON'T QUIT 5 MINUTES BEFORE THE MIRACLE

By: Keegan White

At the beginning of 2019, I attended an intensive keynote speech writing and performing coaching session with my coaches at Heroic Public Speaking.

....

Up until this MOMENT
I had been IGNORING *the signs*
the UNIVERSE *had been sending me*

....

for years to speak on my experience in sobriety from addiction.

I've always known I have a gift for speaking. I'm one of those rare people that actually feels more comfortable on stage then in one on one conversations. You could probably say I was heavily influenced by my mother who was an actress in her younger years. She had me performing in my first play by the age of four and from that point I was hooked!

I signed up for the training to use speaking to reach more people in my life and mindset coaching business. I'm very open about my sobriety and included part of my story of addiction in my speech.

About 3/4ths of the way through the speaker training I was rehearsing my speech with a small group of participants as part of our training. The impact my speech had on them would change the trajectory of my business.

After I spoke, I was overwhelmed by the number of audience members who shared with me that they had family members who had suffered or died from the disease of addiction. In hearing their stories, I realized in that moment that

....

the IMPACT *I was put on this* PLANET
to have would NEVER *be in* LIFE COACHING
but that it would be in SHARING
my STRUGGLE *with addiction and* GETTING
and STAYING SOBER.

....

As I began to navigate this new direction in my business, it wasn't clear exactly what I would be doing… only that I knew I would be speaking about my experience in addiction and sobriety.

Who I would be coaching and on what has continued to evolve with every step that I take. I believe that taking action will give us more information and with that information we can determine what our next step can be. It's when we get stuck in analysis paralysis that we spin our wheels and our energy. We get paralyzed by our thoughts when we either give ourselves too many choices to choose from and then become afraid of making the wrong choice. This is analysis paralysis.

So I kept taking big and small steps to start shifting things in my business. I was so excited! It felt like for the first time since starting my business that I was actually on the right path. Everything up until then felt like I was slightly out of alignment, trying to make it work.

I learned that the Universe will whisper our calling to us again and again until we are ready to step fully into that calling.

I've also learned that even when I exclaimed in front of a room full of people, "this is what I am meant to do with my life!" that eventually that pink cloud of bliss would wear off and the old bugaboos of our self-doubt would creep back into my mind.

From the work that I do with clients, I understand that the self-doubt is what the inner critic uses to keep me safe from stepping out of my comfort zone, even if that means aborting my life's calling.

And that's when the sabotage set in!

It was like as soon as I put my stake in the ground and declared, "this is what I am meant to do with my life!" my subconscious mind took over and declared all out war on keeping me from truly stepping into my life's purpose.

I'm a mindset coach so I'm very familiar with sabotage and how it can creep up at the most inopportune times... like when I'm stepping out of my comfort zone. Even if that comfort zone hasn't felt in alignment.

The sabotage went so far that I started looking for a job.

In all of my years of being an ENTREPRENEUR I had NEVER looked for SOMETHING else because it was NEVER an option.

But I was coming up with all kinds of excuses as to why I needed to get a job with a steady paycheck.

I was tired of the hustle.

I was tired of "having" to be on social media.

I was tired of the inconsistent income.

I was tired of launches.

I was just tired and I was burned out.

So I put aside my dream of speaking, spent time revamping my resume and applied for jobs. I even interviewed and did so well that they immediately asked me to come back for a follow up interview with the hiring manager.

And that's when I had to get honest with myself.

Was I seriously going to go work for someone else nine hours a day, five days a week, having to ask permission for time off, putting my business, freedom, and dreams to the side?

NOPE.

And truthfully, I knew I never was.

But I think I needed to go through that experience so I could come out on the other side appreciating all that comes with being an entrepreneur.

Because it's not always easy running your own business, especially when you are a creative person whose strengths are creating content, teaching and speaking and whose edges are adhering to a self made schedule, marketing, and sales funnels.

The entire time I was revamping my resume and looking for a job I think deep down I knew I wouldn't actually follow through with taking a desk job and quitting my business.

But I had gotten to a place where I resented my business, sales, lead generation, social media and the coaching industry as a whole.

I was burned out and needed the option to make a choice to stay committed to my business and my dreams. Looking for something else gave me that option.

And for me feeling like I have a choice put me back in command of my business.

What I learned from this experience is sometimes in order not to quit, I needed to explore what other options were out there so that I could appreciate what I have created for myself - control of my schedule, freedom to travel, uncapped income, and meaningful and impactful work that helps others make major changes in their own lives.

I also learned not to give up five minutes before the miracle. That's a saying from the 12-step program I used to help me get sober. It means that miracles are right around the corner for you and if you decide to leave early you will miss them.

I've heard it said many times that "entrepreneurship isn't for the faint of heart" and there is definitely truth in that. I showed up to my coaching business with a very high learning curve with my minimal experience in business. It's so easy to watch other coaches or colleagues excel in their businesses and feel like something is wrong with me. That comparison to others robs us of the joy of our own experience and I am certainly guilty of that. When I remember how far I've come from active addiction to getting sober to working at a coffee shop to leading yoga teacher trainings to coaching to speaking, I am overwhelmed with gratitude for what I've been able to accomplish.

It's so easy to look at others around us or on social media to define what success is. For a long time, I associated success with how many clients a person has, how big their business is, how much money they were making or how many social media followers they have. And I compared myself to these people, marking my success by what they were projecting on social media.

One day I had an epiphany. I realized I had never defined what success meant to me and having that revelation gave me so much freedom because it meant I could create my own definition of success.

When I first got sober, just getting through the day without using any drugs or alcohol was a successful day and for a while that was more than enough.

Success is what you make of it based on your needs and where you are in your life. Staying sober has become a way of life for me now so my focus on success has shifted.

Dedicating time to my mental and physical health, family time, rest time, and work on my business are all priorities to me. Every day that I can contribute to those areas are a successful day and depending upon what season or cycle of life I am in will determine how much time and energy goes into each area.

We live in a society that bombards us with messages that you need to look a certain way, have the "right" car and house, your kids need to go to a certain school, and you need to make "X" amount of money. Success is defined for us and many of buy into what marketers tell us because they are really great at their job. Or maybe you are trying to live up to the version of success that your parents taught you.

At the end of the day I invite you to define what success means to you.

By: Keegan White

Hi! I'm Keegan White and I believe that I have been placed on this planet to teach people how to heal. To heal from their patterns, habits, and beliefs that have been holding them back and keeping them stuck.

I am passionate about working with people who have been beat down by their patterns, habits, beliefs and empowering you to break through what has been holding you back.

I began my own spiritual path of healing over a decade ago when I walked into a treatment facility to treat my addiction to drugs, alcohol, and an abusive relationship. (Did you know relationships can be just as addictive and toxic as substances?)

After hitting the lowest point in my life - emotionally, spiritually and mentally - I began my own journey to truly become whole, to reconnect with my body and mind, to heal. As I became more integrated, I began to see the mind, body, and spirit connection as one, my self-esteem began to increase and I no longer craved the destructive habits that had at one time haunted me.

Since experiencing this freedom, my mission has been to educate others on how their patterns, habits, or beliefs are affecting their lives and how to break free, connect with their highest Self, and live a more peaceful and purposeful life.

REFLECT ON YOUR PAST TO UNDERSTAND YOUR PRESENT

By: Robert Wall

What is the one defining moment during your entrepreneurial journey that transformed and changed the trajectory of your life and/or business?

I've decided to answer this question by sharing an extremely vulnerable moment in my life. A moment that may not appear to be part of my entrepreneurial journey, but absolutely became the catalyst in creating the man before you.

I will forever remember this day. Although I had already experienced some success in business and life in general, what I once thought to be my true "WHY" had been disrupted entirely on July 05, 2001. I was doing all the right things, extremely focused on my goals, had two businesses fully operational and in the green, was the youngest in Michigan to become a Chamber of Commerce President, all while being appointed to multiple boards within the community. Success seemed imminent… until I heard those chilling words, "Mr. Wall, if you would, please step out into the hallway".

My beautiful daughter, Elizabeth Ann (Liz), was born on that day, 7 weeks early. This wasn't a huge shock since her big sister was also born premature at 30 weeks, weighing in at a whopping 3lbs. But this was different. Liz wasn't making the sound all parents eagerly anticipate at birth, there wasn't a cry and the only sound filling the room was the medical staff frantically going to work on the apparent situation. Finally! There was that beautiful voice crying out, begging to be put back where she came from (smiling as I type).

They took Liz into another room to tend to her for a while, giving me time to celebrate her birth and recovery with her mother, siblings, and my parents. 30 minutes into the celebration came those forever haunting words again, "Mr. Wall, if you would, please step out into the hallway." A cold chill came across my body, "she's breathing, but requires a little assistance." Thank God! Recognized now as a blessing, I had already been through this before with her sister and felt slightly reassured in this confirmation. They went on to explain, in all their combined experience and in the history of this hospital, they had no idea what they were looking. What??? Liz was born with segmented joints, cataracts, an abnormal skeleton and restricted organs. "Mr. Wall, we are bringing in experts to tell us more," isn't something a parent ever expects to hear on a day that should be celebrated. I had stood on stage in front of thousands, spoke in front of hundreds, sang as a lead vocalist in filled auditoriums, yet nothing has ever been more paralyzing than stepping back into that hospital room to share those findings with my family.

By the end of that day, on July 05, 2001, I was informed that my daughter Elizabeth had RCDP and her life was terminal. I was blessed by God, who entrusted me and her mother with close to 2.5 years of care for her. My little angel Lizzy passed away on October, 22, 2003 (tears).

How did you persevere during this moment?

I cannot say that the journey went smooth. However, in a time where much was lost, a great deal of other things were found. Initially, my business and relationships suffered greatly, but by the grace of God, family, and a few good friends, I somehow found myself climbing out from the dark ascension of emotion I'd fallen into.

> *"It is during our* **DARKEST** *moments that we must* **FOCUS** *to see the* **LIGHT**" *~Aristotle.*

And that is exactly what I did!

What did you learn from the experience?

I learned a great deal from this experience, as I have from all my trials and tribulations, in both life and business. Although cliché, life is way too short to fret the small things. Where being stranded on the side of the road with a flat tire or an unexpected loss of income would have angered me in the past, I no longer allow those events to become anchors in my life or emotions. I have been able to marry both IQ and EQ together, recognizing that most trials in life are magnified by our interpretation of them.

> **SURVIVING** *whatever* **STORM** *you're in,*
> **GREAT** *or* **SMALL,** *is really the* **KEY.**

Don't ever give up; always have faith that the storm shall pass because, even when it has, you may not remember how you endured its beatings. The only certainty I can provide is that the person who comes through the storm has been changed. You'll be stronger, kinder, wiser and more humble than the person you once were walking into the storm.

What did you learn about yourself from this experience?

I could write an entire book on how my experiences have outlined my life, to include all the things I've learned about myself (it just so happens that book is already in process). Reflecting on your past, in order to understand the present, is a difficult exercise to perform at times; you see, I was raised a fighter, literally.

Although involved at a young age in both wrestling and karate, it wasn't until my young adult years, while in the military, that my obsession with martial arts and boxing became my passion. Even more so, I was good at it! I took first place in many tournaments, whether in shootfighting, taekwondo, aikido, or kickboxing, I wanted to be involved in them all. I had been gifted this natural knack of entering a ring, filled with fear, yet simultaneously having the mindset of leaving victorious.

I'm sure my past experiences led me to this point in life, but I'll reserve that for the book. In getting back to my point, burying my daughter was the hardest thing I've ever endured. I allowed myself to become careless, arrogant, driven more by fame and primarily focused on the commas. I was young, in my twenties, managing two profitable businesses, and boastful of my accomplishments and status within the community; quite frankly, I felt unstoppable.

Where did this arrogance come from? Another trait to avoid in business. Remember to always remain authentic and be vulnerable. Risking your thoughts and feelings does not translate to weakness, in fact, the opposite. If you are in control of yourself, better the opportunity you'll have to lead others.

Upon graduating high school, I went straight into the United States Airforce, allowing me to see the world and share in experiences that most people dream of doing. I transitioned quickly from apprentice to project manager, which resulted in me starting my own business within 3 short years. All because somewhere along the line, I bought into the idea that I could build a better mousetrap, that I would crush the competition and, like that fighter in me, I would be leaving the ring victorious! The word "I" is stated too often here, which became relevant as time went on.

Many beautiful relationships and even some miracles developed from Elizabeth's birth as well as her death. Although tragic, I've come to realize that none of this was in vain. In fact, as I too slowly rose from the ashes of my former self, life had new purpose. I became even better at servicing my clients, I had more intent focus. My strength was no longer empowered by the vanity I previously spoke of, but because everything I wanted out of life was no longer just about me. I had a new purpose. My newly developed "WHY" may have included ingredients from the past (Faith, Family, Success), but now served in an entirely new way, placing my clients, partners, and community on the frontline. I now became obsessed with a desire to see others succeed in life!

What do you believe are the most important characteristics and skills one must possess to have a successful life?

I could provide a long list of tools and skillsets to help guide you towards success in both life and business, but here are my primary ones. In no particular order, although each drives the other, in my personal experience and over two decades of working with hundreds of clients, I've found it imperative to focus on Mindset, Heart-set and Faith.

In reflecting back on the loss of my daughter, or even on less important things, such as lost opportunity or financial hardship, I must admit that whether I did or did not recognize it, Mindset was critical. I wouldn't have had the cognitive ability to push through those moments of pain without igniting my brain in a positive manner. Without a positive mindset, it's hard to break out from a negative routine. It's much more than intellectual intelligence, it's having the ability to control your emotional intelligence as well. I've had the privilege of setting up and leading Masterminds all around the world and have come to the realization that we are all our own worst critics.

We criticize everything about ourselves, including image, weight, skills, accolades, and in most cases, we actually hear our own voice in our heads. With this, it's almost impossible to accomplish any goals you've set for yourself. Instead, try to imagine the face and voice of someone you wouldn't dare let down. Every morning, I imagine my wife and children, future looking, telling me how much I mean to them, or thanking me for overcoming the obstacles I've endured to create a better life for them.

Heart-set...

> *now that you've* FOCUSED *on having a* STRONGER MIND, *does it align with your* 'WHY'?

Are you willing to do whatever it takes to have, achieve and deliver, not only to yourself, but to the needs of others? In the end, the product or service I deliver to my clients can only be as big as my belief in bringing joy into their hearts. A large portion of my "WHY" must include helping them with identifying and achieving theirs as well. To be good is skillful, to be great, requires having the passion and desire to help others get what they want.

So, why did I include Faith in my list of skills? I mention God a few times in my writings, so where I stand should be apparent. How, what, or whom you believe is irrelevant. I'm more interested in you having some form of belief, a bigger purpose. I've most recently reminded myself of this, I must place Purpose over Profit. Businesses and households require profit in order to function, so I won't dismiss that. However, being driving by faith, having belief in a higher power, understanding the world and its mission, is much bigger than us. Having your product or service aligned with your values will bring so much more reward to you and others. Faith can move mountains; it can also move your business!

How do you use these skills and characteristics in your home business and for your clients?

I have alluded to the fact that I help organizations or communities create and manage Masterminds. Additionally, although I coach individuals by "starting with the end in mind," I also focus on what happens at the beginning. Most people fail because they've spent their entire time building their business, while overlooking the fact that people buy from people, "those whom they know, like and trust". There is little trust in products or services, unless they feel comfortable with you. Most have forgotten to brand themselves. After all, YOU are the product; YOU are the service.

Whether building a Mastermind or coaching an individual, both require clear direction, a blueprint. This blueprint is custom to the individual, product or service, but always utilizes the 3 core skillsets I've mentioned above.

Through this process of self-branding, you'll acquire a strong foundation in Mindset, Heart-set and Faith, this starts with "Your Story". This helps you to become vulnerable, building authentic rapport and a stronger connection with your audience, clients or customers.

By: Robert Wall

Robert Wall has been a professional business consultant, coach and owner of businesses for over 24 years. He has created, bought, sold and provided turnaround services for a multitude of businesses, ranging from franchise development, family owned businesses, to Fortune 500 companies. Over the past 3 years, Robert started transitioning from traditional consulting to helping his clients launch their businesses and increase their exposure by personally branding themselves online. **"You see, YOU are the brand way before your business is"**. He is an expert at mindset, tapping into ones true passion, while creating a plan to monetize that calling. Robert proudly calls Greenville South Carolina his home, residing with his wife and 3 children (his WHY in life), is originally from Michigan, has traveled globally in his service with the USAF and continues his passion of travel, **"I'm captivated by people, culture, good food and drink"**.

Although he holds his BBA, he credits his success with the entrepreneurial journey he's endured for over two decades. Aside from working diligently for and with his clients, students and business partners, Robert is a musician, a diverse vocalist and speaks nationally regarding subjects on Business, Mindset, Branding, Sales and the development of Masterminds.

Scan me

FOLLOW YOUR PASSIONS TO STAY TRUE TO YOURSELF

By: Kathy Goughenour

My morning routine hasn't changed much since I started my Virtual Assistant (VA) business in 2001. Since then, each morning I wake up, shower, and throw on whatever fun, patterned pair of pajamas call to me that morning. "Wear me, Kathy," they squeal, all vying for the honor to be worn to work that day. I select one and then I choose my headgear: a tiara.

You heard me correctly. This is the life I've created for myself and I adore it. A life where I work from the comfort of my own home – a tiny house in the woods of the Missouri Ozarks – in comfy, crazy pajamas, sporting wild tiaras and doing what I love.

Dressed and ready, I sit down to my desk with a big cup of coffee in hand and descend into the belly of my inbox which has quite the appetite. These days, my email isn't the only thing overflowing. So is my bank account. It hasn't always been like this though.

There was a moment along this journey where the only thing my email seemed to be taking in and spitting back out were messages of "we are no longer in need of your services." My client base went from 70 to 25 in only 30 days. Every morning, sitting down to check emails my spirit sunk a little lower and my blood pressure raised a little higher. Every time a client wrote to say they had to end our contract, I saw them walk out of my proverbial office with big fat bills attached to their backs, closing the door behind them. If they were leaving, so was the money.

I had been doing well enough for myself up until then. I had made a six-figure business out of being a Real Estate Virtual Assistant – performing a variety of marketing functions for the agents I worked with - and nearly doubled what I had made in my corporate job. This was after my boss, a man who wouldn't promote me because I smiled and laughed too much, told me when I resigned that I was making the biggest mistake of my life. That I would never make the money I had been making there. There I was seven years later, having become successful from my own hard work and determination and yet was staring at my screen morning after morning, watching clients fall away. Money leaving with them.

It wasn't anything I had done. The circumstances were well beyond my control. It was 2008. The year the real estate bubble burst. The housing market crashed. The financial crisis bloomed. That March, more than 400 defendants were charged with mortgage fraud. The same month my email inbox started delivering termination letters.

While losing 70% of my client base and income was already a tough pill to swallow, my husband and I lost $500,000 in mutual funds as a result of what was happening across the country. Our hard-earned retirement funds were gone in a snap. All that loss produced a great deal of fear.

You know they say with fear there are three responses: fight, flight, or freeze. Well, I was a flight-er. At least then. Staring at that much income swirl down the drain, I reacted in a hurry. I sold the remaining part of my business to another VA who was intending to stick it out. Then, I decided I was going to go back to the one thing I knew I could do and where I had the feeling (false though I now know it was) of security: a traditional job working for someone else.

I found a position that was brilliantly aligned with the work I had been doing as a Virtual Assistant: an executive assistant to the President of a local college. Determined to get this job, I did all the things you're supposed to do, including paying professionals to redo my résumé, and calling around asking my contacts to talk me up. This town was small. A town I knew intimately. I had all the right people in all the right places (including the mayor's wife and many on the college's board!) calling on my behalf.

Heck, I even spoke to the person who was leaving the position and they passed on my name as their recommendation. If there was a book called "How to Get a Job," I followed it to the letter. With powerful work experience, an MBA, a polished résumé, and great connections, I just had to get this job. There was no reason not to. When I had put my mind to leaving my original corporate job, I had been successful. Certainly, it worked in reverse, right? Put your mind to something and go. But the Universe knew more than I did (*thankfully*).

You know what that means, don't you? I didn't get it.

I didn't even get an interview. Instead, a form letter (read: rejection) arrived in the mail. Through my connections, I learned they hired a twenty-three-year-old who didn't even have an Associate degree. While we all know that discrimination based on age is illegal, we also all know that it's real and it happens. It wasn't lost on me that as a fifty-one-year-old woman with an MBA, I may have been overlooked for being too old and too qualified.

While that rejection should have been enough to remind me of why I left Traditional Job Land to begin with, it wasn't. So, I applied to yet another position at a different school, going through all the same steps as before. Again, I didn't get an interview. This time I didn't even get a form letter. Instead, the recruiter for the position told me in passing that the college wasn't interested because, "The only thing you've done [in the last seven years] is work for yourself." I swallowed my anger and resisted the temptation to defend the career I had made for myself, but the sting of those words was a second slap in the face.

That is what did it. The shake I needed from the Universe to wake up. "Earth to Kathy, don't you remember who you are? What you're capable of?" There was this feeling of reawakening after being stuck in a nightmare. I remembered why I had gone out on my own to begin with. And I promised myself that no matter how bad it got ever again; I would never return to work for someone else.

This internal recognition was the easy part. I still needed to figure out how to recoup my losses and re-establish a business, especially now that I had sold what remained of the one, I had. The looming question, "What do I do now?" hung overhead.

I had one idea. One idea that had been playing softly in the back of my mind for about a year: the idea to develop a training program. While I had run my Real Estate VA business, I had trained five people as subcontractors to help me carry the load. There wasn't anyone to hire at the time who met my standards for being proactive, a great problem-solver, and professional. So, I trained these women for free and realized how much I loved teaching them. I discovered I enjoyed teaching women (also unhappy with their work lives) how to become empowered and confident women, superheroes of their own success, by building successful Virtual Assistants businesses from their homes. With nothing else to lose, I created the program and then went through it myself to ensure it was successful.

Using the methods, I developed, within 60 days I had determined a new target market, contracted with 7 new clients, and was on my way to $75K annually working from home as a VA for professional speakers. By September of 2008, I enrolled people in my first Expert VA Training session. From 2008-2015, I only enrolled about eight people a year. I didn't market heavily; it was all word of mouth. But from the get-go there was so much fulfillment from it, so much joy. Still, I treated it like a side-project, a part-time gig, and I continued to work as a VA for professional speakers on the side, filling in my income gaps as needed.

Then in 2015, a business coach said to me that until I chose one business to truly devote my time, energy, and attention to, I would never really be giving 100% to either – the training program or the speakers. In order to grow one of these, I needed to choose one to nurture. I needed to only have a Plan A to focus on. No Plan B. So, I was at a crossroads: choose working solely with professional speakers as a VA or choose to turn my training program into a full-time business.

My heart was always fullest when I was coaching and training, so that same year (2015), I dropped the speakers I had and went all-in on my coaching program. With the support of a business coach, I started to focus on taking bigger risks, resulting in bigger rewards. Truly, the most beautiful thing has resulted. This Expert VA Training program is the one I am now known for and it changes women's lives for the better all over North America.

It's also significantly changed my life and my revenue. In 2016 and 2017 I reached 100K just from my training and coaching biz. In 2018 I brought in 300K. And for 2019, I'm on track for one million! I have 50 new students currently enrolled in the program, 14 going through the second-level coaching to reach six-figures, and six going through the top-tier mastermind-level to reach multiple six-figures. There are 1,300 in my "closed" Expert VA Community Facebook group, 150 Alumni in my "secret" Facebook group. And eight coaches leading all these troops in addition to running their own businesses; two of my coaches were some of my very first students back in 2008. I was just featured in Forbes, and I'm a part of several women's masterminds. I get to rub elbows with some of the best and most brilliant leaders, thinkers, and visionaries across a variety of industries working to matchmake them to their perfect Expert VAs® and Virtual Experts®.

I get to travel. I get asked to do interviews on podcasts. I speak live on stages. I run my own annual live event exclusively for VAs (during which we have nightly PJ Parties for VIPs). I'm working on my first book. I've recouped all that I lost in 2008 and then some, and I can't even believe that this is my life.

In following my passion and staying true to myself and my values, I've created not just a training program that teaches new skills or impacts my students' bottom line, but that creates a community of remarkable, powerful women who are truly there to lift each other up and cheer each other on.

While I went through real devastation and panic in 2008 as a result of what the housing crash did to my business, I am grateful. While the feelings of rejection and worthlessness after two failed attempts to return to the workplace were disheartening, I am grateful. Those two rejections reminded me of the time and place when I was in a corporate job with no hope or joy and the loss of both had propelled me to jump on the entrepreneurial journey to begin with. Faced again with a similar joy-less and hope-less circumstance, I rediscovered my strength.

Running back to what I knew out of fear wasn't the answer. From that moment, I made an eternal vow to never doubt myself ever again. I re-found my internal voice and determination that I could create my own destiny.

From that place of loss and rejection, was an impenetrable decision to succeed. To not take "no" from anyone. To keep going. To never give up. No matter the obstacle, there is a solution. I learned if there was a problem you couldn't go *through*, then you found a way to go *around* instead.

I learned how to have an abundance mindset and to face down fear. An abundance mindset allows me to look at risks as fun and rewarding rather than scary. If I believe there is an abundance of opportunity, wealth, results, etc. I don't have to fear not making it. There is enough on the other side, no matter what.

Over the course of time, I have developed two powerful principles by which I live my life and speak to everything else:

1) Run your business the way you want to run your life.

2) Fun and joyfulness are not just reserved for home or for work, it's to be felt at both.

And, more than anything else, I've come to believe, see, feel and model that what one woman can do, another can do.

By: Kathy Goughenour

After finding the courage to say "bye-bye" to her corporate marketing career, Kathy Goughenour built a 6-figure virtual assistant business from her tiny house in the middle of a forest. Today, she teaches professional women how to create their own work-at-home VA businesses so they can enjoy the freedom, flexibility and financial

security they desire and deserve. Kathy also offers free VA Matchmaking sessions to business owners interested in working with high-quality Expert VAs. Kathy and her Expert VA Training program have been featured in Forbes, HuffPost, Good Housekeeping, All You, and The Wealthy Freelancer. For more information, visit <u>www.expertvatraining.com</u>

MY GIFT TO YOU - FROM TRAUMA TO HAHA

By: Maude Bombardier

Six months after launching my business, my darkest secret was resurfacing. A secret I convinced myself had no effect on the strong woman I am, a secret I had tried to bury for the last 23 years of my life, a secret I didn't understand as a child – an event of child abuse at the age of 7. While you might wonder how my story made its way in an entrepreneurial book, it has all the reasons to be here. Let me explain why and share my takeaways for uncovering childhood trauma as a solo entrepreneur in a start-up company. I want my story to be one of inspiration, of lessons learned, and of resourcefulness to you.

My life's mission was always one of inspiring a positive mindset and sharing healthy coping strategies. For years, I knew I wanted to work in the field of education, positive psychology, and public speaking. It therefore didn't come as a surprise to my friends and family when I launched *The Laughing Hour* in 2018, a unique team-bonding experience through laughter. After only a couple of months, I had already been featured on various television news channels, a podcast, a blog, and in online news articles across Canada in both French and English. I felt as if a star was aligning everything in my favour. I had found my calling. I thought my business was going to be a story of success with absolutely no dipping points, making some sort of extraordinary statement. Life laughed at this idea. Here is what happened instead.

The human body is fascinating, and our brains are quite wise. A child who experiences a traumatic event is not at an age to process the information with the adequate coping mechanisms to understand what happened and deal with it. I have learnt that very often (but not in all cases) the brain of these children put the memories in a box and hide them. Over time, the dust accumulates as the well-kept secret stays there, making no noise. It's patiently waiting for a moment where the individual is stable and mentally capable of dealing with the facts. That moment for me was six months after launching my business. Memories of my childhood trauma started creeping its way back in my head and for the first time in my life I felt the crying urge to let it out.

As I started seeking therapy and peeling layers off, I went through waves of emotions. I experienced moments of rage, hyperventilating as tears flooded my eyes, swearing in total disgust. I was easily irritable and wanted to hide in my room in need of being in my own bubble. I got angry at my partner for wanting to invite friends over to our home, feeling they were entering my safe space. I often felt like staying alone as the only answer that came to mind when I was asked "What's new with you?" was "My child abuse counsellor and I met this week."

Imagine waking up knowing you need to facilitate a laughing workshop for twenty, fifty, sometimes even hundreds of people while in the midst of uncovering a childhood trauma. As if that wasn't enough, I was also hosting a weekly happiness radio capsule on positive psychology studies to inspire an optimistic mindset. I danced in my head with the idea I was being dishonest and a liar to my clients and audience. I felt as though I was an intruder and inauthentic, even though I know I am meant to be a happiness catalyst. As a result, I began doubting myself and became scared of success. I thought success in today's world with vulnerability being popularized meant I would need to share my everyday struggles publicly to be authentic. I was terrified, yet curiously fascinated as a growing understanding of decisions I had made in my life suddenly made sense. If each emotion would be on a color scale from anger to pure blissfulness, I can assure you my days where filled with rainbows. And what's fascinating with rainbows is that you need the sun and rain to be able to enjoy them.

I believe there is beauty in all aspects of my life, not always easily understandable in moments of crisis, but definitely there waiting for me to unpack it and take the opportunity to see the best in the situation. You live, you fail, you grow, and you rise. It's important to mention that there's no beauty in the actions of my abuser, but I believe there is beauty in how I am rising during my healing. I want to share with you what helped me apart from therapy: my daily gifts, and laughter.

The beauty and irony of me uncovering my childhood trauma in my first year of launching my business was that I was literally getting paid to get a taste of my own medicine – laughter wellness. I was being hired to facilitate laughing experiences that were more beneficial to me than my clients could have ever imagined. After every laughing session, I would feel like myself again. I would be more productive. I was more focused. I would sing in the car. I felt relaxed and alive.

The technique I use to facilitate these workshops is laughter yoga, where laughter sparks from within rather than from an external stimulus. I don't tell jokes. I don't dress like a clown. I simply encourage individuals to start laughing for absolutely no reason. Yes, it feels awkward and weird. Even more so while not being in the mood to laugh. It does require some stepping out of your comfort zone, but as entrepreneurs we are required to step out of our comfort zone constantly. That's where the magic happens, and in the case of laughter yoga that's when the benefits occur.

The science behind this laughter yoga technique is that your brain can't tell the difference between a real laugh and a forced laugh. The benefits are therefore the same. When participants use their bodies to trick their brain into thinking they are having a blast, their brain responds by secreting endorphins and serotonin – which is basically a happiness cocktail in my world. The list of laughter benefits is huge (increase productivity, social connections, immune system booster to name a few), but the best part for myself was the shift I felt inside me during each session. From feeling out of place when I began facilitating my laughing workshops to feeling at peace and rejuvenated when the session ended is an indescribable feeling that anyone in distress craves for.

As strongly as I believe in the benefits of laughter, I don't believe in one singular ultimate solution to all problems. I believe in the benefits of mixing and matching various coping strategies as an all-time modulator to make stressful events manageable. I believe what will personally help an individual release some stress one day might produce anxiety another day. In some cases, laughter brought me anxiety and annoyed me more than I would care to admit. That's where my second practice came into play.

A well-balanced life is important for me. As an entrepreneur, hustling is a common mindset that individuals tend to pride themselves on, but here's something you need to remember. Hustling only goes so far without inner peace and self-care. I came across numerous psychology studies in the book *The How of Happiness* by Sonja Lyubomirsky that confirmed the extent of a practice I had developed for myself to help my inner peace – my daily gift checklist. Call it whatever you want: gifts, stress management, self-care – it all boils down to the same essence. Every day (or most days as I am human) it is important for me to know that I am gifting myself a moment. The importance is not how long the moment is but rather that I deliberately and consciously made the decision that a moment is MY GIFT of the day. As I was uncovering my childhood trauma, I had mornings where I woke up with a cloud and rain in my head. Asking myself the question "What is your daily gift today, Maude?" helped me get out of bed. It's the simple things in life that bring most joy, and my checklist was a compilation of simple activities that made me smile – no grandiose activities needed.

At times, what I felt would bring me the most joy was to walk around the house saying good morning to my plants. On cold snowy days, I sometimes made the decision to listen to a bird soundtrack to feel as if it was summer. When I was driving to facilitate a Laughing Hour, I made the decision to turn off the radio in the car and repeat my motivational speech loud and proud. I even added Spanish on my checklist at one point just for the heck of it as listening to Spanish tutorial podcasts made me feel good. My checklist was therefore flexible and changed with time. It's important to note that none of the daily gifts on the list were goals I was striving to accomplish. I was not intentionally trying to learn Spanish at that moment, therefore the thought of not doing it one day did not create any feelings of guilt.

I am a fervent believer that every day is a gift which should be celebrated. Whatever a daily gift represents to you, whatever helps you rise joy, whatever brings you peace and happiness – the simple fact you took some time for yourself is worth celebrating and putting a smile on.

If there is one takeaway I wish to inspire from my story, it's to continuously equip yourself with stress management strategies. Stress management strategies is a fancy term, but it doesn't need to be a complicated acronym or concept, because complicated concepts don't do good in moments of distress. You need to know your go-to's in times of crisis in order to turn towards a healthy coping behaviour and not a destructive one.

To help make my point valid, I would like for you to imagine you live in a beautiful home. You enter your kitchen one day and there's a leak in the sink. My question to you is what is more efficient? Having no tools whatsoever in and around your house? Or running around to find duct tape in hope to find some and crossing your fingers that it will magically help the leak? Or knowing exactly where your toolkit is and what tools will best fix the problem? I don't know for you, but I vote for the last option.

The way we deal with issues in our lives, small or big, personal or in our businesses, should be the same. In an ideal world, we would own all the tools and know how to repair everything. That is obviously not the case – at least, not for me! But by actively and consciously learning what helps permanently fix our own personal leaks, not just temporarily with duct tape, we are maintaining a strong healthy home.

A very easy exercise you can do is to create a list of possible go-to's in moments of crisis. I know for me, at times when I was the most stressed, I would need to lock myself up and cry, then go for a run or dance, followed by journaling or brainstorming solutions or figuring out the bigger meaning of whatever had manifested in my life. This package worked wonders many times, but it was not necessarily always the best set of tools to fix all life challenges. Just as much as duct tape can fix many problems, it isn't the best suited solution for a kitchen leak. Some days, laughter was the best suited tool to help me. Other days, a talk with my therapist was greatly needed. So, make an inventory of your tools and know what types of damages they can help fix. Get the help of a professional plumber if you need to, or attend a plumbing class if you want to learn something new.

Whatever it is that you need to fix in your home, I want you to know there is a giant within you waiting for you to peel off the layers and rise up to the challenge of standing tall and free. I'm still in the process of uncovering these layers. There will always be some fixes and good old maintenance to do in my home. But that's what owning a home is and that's what being human and alive is. My healing process is not done, and I don't expect to have a prize at the end. Healing is a journey and during this journey there are days of all sorts, some sunnier than others and some with many rainbows. I might as well be celebrating them with daily gifts, laughter, and with those that matter while doing what I love.

Special Note: This chapter is dedicated to my therapist, Deborah. After struggling with my chapter for a month, you told me two words that inspired me to write the chapter in a couple of hours – growth mindset. Thank you!

A driven optimist on a mission to sparkle joy everywhere she goes, Maude Bombardier is the founder of The Laughing Hour. Launched in 2018, her company offers a unique team-building experience increasing productivity, effective communication, and stress management through... laughter!

By: Maude Bombardier

Maude's passion for promoting well-being goes beyond The Laughing Hour. This entrepreneur and first-time author graduated with a degree in Psychology at Bishop's University after studying for two years in Early Childhood and Elementary Education at Concordia University. She had a French happiness radio capsule that aired weekly in Edmonton, Canada where she talked about various scientific studies suggesting how to flourish happiness in your own life.

A strong believer in giving back, Maude sits on the board of directors of a French sports federation in Alberta, and volunteers at Pilgrims Hospice, an end-of-life facility that brings compassionate care to their patients and their caregivers.

She does not pretend she's a happiness expert, but rather an eternal student that loves sharing and learning on the subject of laughter, well-being, and a balanced life.

PS. Maude is pronounced like "Beast Mode" or "Happy Mode".
Website: www.TheLaughingHour.com
Email: info@TheLaughingHour.com
Facebook: www.facebook.com/TheLaughingHour
Instagram: @The_LaughingHour or @Maude.Bombardier
Freebie: https://www.thelaughinghour.com/motivation

Scan me

SIMPLIFY TO MULTIPLY

By: Joy Bufalini

I was angry. No, not just angry. I was angry and determined. I picked up the pillow from our bed and threw it across the room along with a few choice words.

My husband Brian remembers that summer evening conversation well. After 4 years of being a business owner, I was beyond frustrated with how little money I was making. I had been working hard and had been trying so many different strategies to get more clients, but I didn't have many clients and I didn't make more than $20K a year. We had some debt and extra expenses because we have a special needs child, and our life was just getting more expensive with three teenagers. I either had to double my income quickly or go get a job working for someone else.

That evening during the "pillow-throwing" conversation, I decided I was going to turn the status quo around and make my business a success. Something shifted inside of me. I went from "I hope this will work someday" to "I'm doing this now". Instead of wishing and hoping, I moved into 100% decision.

But before I could change my outward results, I had to get honest with myself about what I was doing that wasn't working. I had been spending a lot of time on things that "seemed" like marketing activities, but truthfully were just busy work. I also had been spending a lot of time giving away things for free - free webinars, free videos, free coaching calls – but I didn't have a very intentional strategy to bring in new clients with what I was doing. Plus, I was doing so many different random strategies, and everything seemed complicated. Truth be told, I was really good at implementing simple strategies and getting results in other areas of life. All I needed to do was look back on the 10 years before I became a business owner to see that.

It was 2000 and I was finishing up my last year of teaching middle school and I was very pregnant with boy/girl twins. We had just bought our first home and I was in baby bliss. But 10 weeks before they were due, I went to the doctor to check out what seemed to be a minor symptom and ended up delivering the twins by emergency C-section just a few hours later. After birth, our daughter suffered a severe hemorrhage of the brain which caused significant damage. She was later diagnosed with cerebral palsy which impaired her development of speech and movement. It was a very overwhelming and traumatic time. I realized that I would never go back to teaching as life had taken a very different turn.

At a neurodevelopmental evaluation when our daughter was two, the doctor said that based on the extent of her brain damage and the fact that she was still at an infant level at age 2, she would probably never walk or talk. Being an educator and also a high-achiever, that was not acceptable to me. I went into researcher mode and developed a plan of action to rehabilitate her and defy the doctor's grim prognosis. I consulted other experts who were at the leading edge of brain development and created a research-based schedule of 50 hours a week of very specific therapies. This plan was implemented by her early intervention therapists, people I hired and trained, and my husband and I implemented daily as well. I also acquired $30,000+ in grant money to pay for it all – which required a ton of determination and focus to see it all through.

By age 5, our daughter was walking with a walker and then independently with crutches by age 7. By age 8, she said her first words and could read hundreds of words by pointing to word cards. By age 10, I was able to get her into an excellent school that used a similar philosophy of learning and she was able to continue her progress there. The next year, in 2011, I started my business.

In reflecting back on what I had done in those 10 years with my daughter, I could see that I was clear and focused and was able to carry out a very specific strategy because I had a very strong sense of urgency. I had a very deep "why" that enabled me to focus and use my natural strengths to help my daughter walk and talk, even when the experts had said it was impossible. All I needed to do was bring that same model of thinking into my business.

Here's the interesting thing that shifted after that "line-in-the-sand" conversation with my husband that summer evening. I actually "knew" exactly what I needed to do to move the needle forward quickly. I wrote down the big action steps on a piece of notebook paper and then put it on my bookshelf not to be found until 3 years later inside of a book. It didn't matter because I didn't need to keep looking at my list. I was clear on what I needed to do and I did it. I had "the way" inside of me already.

Within 24 months I grew to multiple six figures and through the process my signature body of work, Simplify to Multiply, was born. Simplify to Multiply is a very specific Method and Mindset that enables you to scale your business quickly without long sales calls, complicated sales funnels, or Facebook ads. Below are a few of the Simplify to Multiply Mindset principles, which are a part of what I now call "The Laws of Income Acceleration". These will help you shift into a new paradigm of thinking and make a quantum leap in your business.

Everything you need is already inside of you

"The way" to significantly multiply your income and impact is already inside of you. Once you are in 100% decision that you are going to do this, then you can actually see the way. A door opens in your mind and suddenly you can see ideas and opportunities that were there all along that you couldn't see them until you were "all in" on your decision. You get resourceful and ask questions. You start tapping into your natural strengths and talents that were previously untapped. You find a way to hire that coach or expert to help you see the next steps. The ability is there once you fully own your desire and your decision.

Everything is a choice

Whether you stay in frustration and dissatisfaction or choose a different path is always your choice. This can be a tough pill to swallow at first because our natural tendency is to point to circumstances outside of ourselves to say "why" we can't do this or that right now or why things are not working out the way we want them to. But the true key to big growth is to take 100% ownership of our reality no matter what is going on in life or business. We always have a choice about which road of thinking we go down. How we think determines the results we get. Realizing that you always have a choice is game-changing.

Desire and commitment have to be stronger than fear

If you are growing and stretching your comfort zone, it's going to feel scary. There's just no way around this. The reason is that it's your unconscious mind's job is to keep you protected emotionally. It tries keep the status quo at all times and it triggers feelings of fear when you do anything where the outcome is uncertain, there are unknown variables, or it's unfamiliar territory. Well that describes about everything you do as an entrepreneur! The key here is to keep tapping into the desire for what you want and your commitment to the next level of growth. Strong desire and commitment will help you get through the inevitable fear.

Priorities determine how quickly you grow

When I look behind the scenes at the business structure of most entrepreneurs, they have followed conventional wisdom in doing what I call "All. The. Things." They have complicated sales funnels, they post on a gazillion different platforms, they are trying to run Facebook ads and/or spending their precious time and energy on strategies that aren't necessarily getting them to their goals. When the business structure is built very wide horizontally, it's as if they have what I call a "two-story high maintenance condo building". Unfortunately, maintaining that business model is a lot of work and a slow path to the big growth that you truly desire. Instead, when you prioritize just a few simple strategies that move the needle forward quickly, you build a gorgeous skyscraper of a business that is strong and sustainable. Once you are making $10K, $20K months and beyond, you can easily hire out help if you want to pursue some of the more complex strategies. The key to quick growth is to prioritize first the things that will bring you a lot of clients and cash without a ton of effort.

Whether you are you are just starting out in business or you've been at it a long time, now is the time to simplify the model you have, prune the things that don't give you much ROI, and create that beautiful skyscraper of a business that will be strong and sustainable for years to come. You'll enjoy your business more and you'll be able to multiply your income and impact more quickly without getting overwhelmed or burning out.

By: Joy Bufalini

Joy Bufalini is an award-winning coach for women entrepreneurs who has been featured in both Entrepreneur and O magazines. She helps her clients to simplify their business model so that they can quickly move to multiple six figures and beyond while doing their genius work and serving their dream clients.

She has turned conventional wisdom on its head through her signature Simplify to Multiply philosophy of "doing less while earning more". She teaches a very specific Method and Mindset that enables her clients to quickly multiply their income while honoring their time and energy. You can find her online at www.joybufalini.com

Joy 10x'd her business after being stuck at a plateau of $20K/year trying to do "all the growth strategies" at once. Once she learned to simplify and to think differently, she quickly scaled to $250K+/year in less than 24 months even with a very full of life with three teenagers, including her special needs daughter Amber.

One of Joy's signature teachings is her Soul-centered Sales process that makes it easy for your dream clients to lean in and say "How do I get started?" without any long sales calls or arm-twisting. To download your guide right now and to connect with Joy, go to www.joybufalini.com.

Scan me

LUCY, THE GREMLIN

By: Evala Rahm

Have you ever been just going about your business, maybe cleaning your house or reading a book, on a beautiful afternoon with the sun streaming in the windows when you get a phone call? Now imagine if the caller ID showed your local county jail? First you might think it's a scam or the wrong number but decide to pick it up anyway.

"Hello?"

How would you feel if the next thing you heard was, "Mom, it's me."?

That was me not so long ago. I was finishing up a contentious divorce (I think both of us are much happier now). I had been a stay-at-home mom and spouse for about twenty-three years. Both of my children battled their own demons during that stressful period of transition. And after several years of legal, financial, emotional and logistical battles, I was trying to come to terms with a lot of shame with my behavior as a parent and a partner. That on top of being a single mom and needing to support my family in every aspect including financially.

The only thing I was sure of was that I wanted to help people avoid the pitfalls that I had jumped into and come out the other side stronger. But how do I do that? I didn't have a clue where to begin! Wait a minute...I know...I'll be a coach! And people will pay me for my advice. Easy-peasy, right?

I proudly hold a VERY OLD Master's degree in counseling but, at that time, hadn't been in the professional world for about 20 years other than some part-time jobs here and there. I loved the idea of coaching because it is so action-based and puts a lot of speed into forward moving direction. Clients learn about SMART goals and do homework. They are challenged to be personally accountable while I get to ask powerful questions and get to the root of what is blocking their progress. And best of all, the clients are actually in charge of the direction of their life. And, I don't really give advice, even when clients ask for it. I just help them find their own solutions that will work best. I love coaching.

But what kind of coach? I first thought I could help others going through the divorce process. But then I changed to recovery coaching. I have been free from alcohol and drugs for over 30 years surely, I have a wealth of knowledge to share. But then, after more soul-searching, I was able to see where my skills, knowledge and expertise would be most useful. The relationship that I had with my children when they were teenagers suffered because of the parenting skills I had at the time. THAT…is where I thought I could be of the most service. So, I became a coach for parents of teenagers who hire me to get them through those years of worry, rage, fear and sometimes joyful pride with some sense of sanity and sense of humor.

My self-esteem was pretty much in the toilet when the divorce wrapped up. I didn't know who I was anymore or even how I had gotten there. And that low self-image, filled with all sorts of catabolic energy, was and continues to be an obstacle for my business! That fear-based gremlin (I named her Lucy) talked down to me all the time. She said things like:

"Who do you think you are? You need a license, PHD, following, etc, to be successful. And   YOU don't have that."

"Everyone has problems with their kids. What makes you so special?"

"Parents don't need you. They can look up answers on the internet."

"You need a real job with health insurance and benefits."

As an entrepreneur, I would say my gremlin was, and still can be, the PRIMARY BLOCK TO MY BUSINESS SUCCESS. When I let that sink in, it was like a light switch flipped on. Ohh… if I want to be successful in business and as a leader to others, I have to learn how to turn my thoughts and beliefs into something useful for me. Those harmful thoughts had been there most of my life. Even though I was not where I had fantasized I would be in life, the idea of changing myself to get there was a total fright fest. I knew that I was going to have to get vulnerable and expose my soft underside to have the kind of business and life I really wanted.

My gremlin, Lucy, threw a huge temper tantrum about it. Except at some point, something inside of me had shifted. Lucy was no longer throwing angry shade at me but expressing real fear. And she was now including me in her outbursts:

"But what if we fail?"

"What if no one likes us?"

"What if we end up alone in a refrigerator box?"

We?? So, Lucy and I became a team. We became one. And on our journey, we had some dragons to fight. Once I acknowledged that Lucy was just trying to protect me, I was able to tell myself that yes, this is a risk, but it is the only way to succeed. I had enough faith that no matter what, if I was working with the intention of helping others get through the rough spots, everything was going to be alright.

I enrolled in coaching school. During that time, I did a lot of personal inventory taking. I realized that just because I thought a certain way, it didn't mean that those thoughts were the "truth". I learned about how my perspective came from all the experiences in my life up to the present moment. And I learned that my perspective acted like a filter so it was not possible to make objective decisions until I was able to look at things from outside my box. In turn, my perspective effected how I acted. Or, in some cases, how I didn't act. And that landed me (and Lucy) exactly where we were…scared to move and scared to stay the same.

A fellow coach shared with me that if I became actively aware of my thoughts, then I would be able to start changing them. I couldn't change what I didn't know. My choices based on those assumptions, interpretations and limiting beliefs might be familiar and habitual but they also blocked me from having the life I dreamed of. However, I found that I could replace my old, useless thoughts with new ones based on fresh evidence and I was able to find peace. So, I learned to evaluate how much of what was happening was empirical and how much of it was my clouded filter. It wasn't long before I was making conscious decisions and a sense of freedom came upon me. It was powerful.

You might ask how I was able to do this. Well, I learned that when I let a few other people in on my secret world, I found out they had some of the same fears that I did. We had a common humanity. I allowed them to see the real me and they liked me for the very things that I thought were weaknesses like crying when I was sad or hurt. And not only were we able to acknowledge and validate each other's thoughts and feelings, we were also able to support each other to make the changes necessary to reach our goals.

I signed up for some marketing classes to improve my knowledge of how to get myself and my business out there. I hired a coach and joined a Mastermind group. A Mastermind is a group of people who have the same basic goal who meet regularly to hold each other accountable, share knowledge and resources and work together as a team in a non-judgmental way. That group still meets monthly to support each other.

As I learned more about myself and more about how to run my business, my self-esteem improved. It really is an internal job.

While it is easy to write this because the big parts of the struggle are behind me, sometimes there is a sticky emotional residue that shows up. You know how when you have a bandage on for several days, through washings and sleep and all sorts of activity and it stays right there? Then you try to take it off and it actually hurts a little and some of the adhesive stays stuck on your skin? That is what happened to my gremlin, Lucy.

I realized that I needed her for many years to survive. I always planned for the worst-case scenario just to have all my bases covered. I always prepared for someone to laugh at me or say something mean. I often lived in a place of fear and tried to intellectualize it away. Here is what I learned:

- People will laugh and be mean but that is their issue, not mine.
- I am exactly where I am supposed to be right here, right now.
- It takes more energy to guess the future, avoid emotional pain and cover all my bases than it does to accept what comes and work in the moment
- That when I work in the moment, I am happier and much more fun to be around

Lucy hung around long enough to get me to adulthood but then I had a hard time taking the protective cover she provided off. And when I finally did it it hurt, a lot, and there was still some residue left. I felt exposed and vulnerable. Yuck! By the time my wounds (fears, hurts and resentments) healed, Lucy also healed and now is just a tiny voice that just needs a little listening. I don't want her to completely go away. She is like the scar under the bandage to remind me of my old life and how far I have come.

Today, when fear pops up, it has the potential to sidetrack me. But I want to thrive. I know that to get new clients, I need to get more public exposure. I recently moved to another state and my coach suggested going to local school events and speaking. What do I do? I take a deep breath, remind myself of my purpose, trust that it is going to be OK and pick up the phone.

Becoming accustomed to my new filter has taken years of practice. I am mindful that in any endeavor worthy of my effort, if failure happens, I still got out there in the face of fear. That is called courage. Every successful keynote speaker, every TED talker, every inspirational podcast or book sends the same message. Failure is important to my success process.

I am grateful for all of the opportunities I have to grow emotionally, spiritually, mentally, physically and financially. Because of them, I am able to express empathy and compassion for my clients. Not only can I help them work through logistical and practical matters when it comes to reaching goals, but I can be a supportive cheerleader in addition to being the coach. I can give my clients a boost of faith when they might not have it themselves. My clients can go to bed at night free to dream of all the possibilities the new day will bring.

By: Evala Rahm

Evala Rahm works with professional parents who feel confused and frustrated by the hormonal, defiant spirit that has possessed their teenagers. She has experienced her own journey into the abyss of parenting through the teenage metamorphosis and come out wiser and stronger with common sense still intact. While this period in life may seem overwhelming and out-of-control, Evala is determined to help families stay out of jail, restore their sanity and serenity while maintaining a sense of humor along the way.

In addition to holding a Master's degree in Counseling, an accreditation with the International Coach Federation, Certification as a Daring Way™ Facilitator, work within the addiction recovery community for over 35 years, Evala has a wealth of hard-earned life experience badges she brings to the table. Ultimately, this gives her clients the most non-judgmental, support environment to explore, clarify and practice living aligned with values that bring them connection and comfort with themselves. Check out my website is www.evalarahm.com to book a free 15 minute strategy session there or through FB at Evala Rahm Coaching OR scan the QR code below.

EMPOWER. GROW. SUCCEED. INSPIRE THROUGH LEARNING.

By: Isla Brook

1. What is the one defining moment during your entrepreneurial journey that transformed and changed the trajectory of your life and/or business?

The one defining moment during my entrepreneurial journey that transformed and changed the trajectory of my life and business was when I hit rock bottom. In a matter of months, I lost my marriage, my home and my corporate job all while I was on maternity leave. I had two small children to support and I had to make a choice and figure out a way to change my situation. I decided to launch a new business and started learning as much as I could online about how to grow and market online. I wanted to utilize all of my professional skills and business skills and be able to serve and help others. So, I started Coaching women in business to build from my previous expertise with a product-based business. Through learning online and reaching out to other entrepreneurs who then became mentors I put together the information I needed to build and grow my business. From here I ended up consulting to online entrepreneurs, inc500 companies and corporate businesses around all key strategic elements of business. This led me to create my own Executive (Virtual) Assistant Academy teaching people everything I know. Going through this challenged me to step into my power and reclaim my inner strength. It made me realize just how strong I was and that I could, in fact, get through really hard times. When you lose everything, you realize what is important and what you actually want in life and you let go of everything that isn't that. I worked every moment I could to build my business, it isn't an overnight story and it takes time but I realized that it is a long term game.

2. How did you persevere during this moment?

I realized that I had to be my own hero and that I needed to back myself 100%. I had to keep fighting for my dreams. I did this through working on my mindset every single day. Reading positive affirmations, growth mindset and personal development books. Following other people's journeys that had been in similar situations inspired me to keep going and to know that my dreams were possible. I knew that it was up to me to get myself out of this situation and that I was going to do this by creating a successful business from home so that I could still have quality time with my children. I also went to networking events and met other people in online groups and conferences that were like-minded. Creating connections with other entrepreneurs that were on similar journeys to me really gave me the support circle I needed. I worked out what I wanted and didn't want in my life and stayed true to this. I created a vision board of my passions, goals and vision. I then created achievable outcome, goals and projects from this list, broke them down into weekly and daily tasks and got to work. I found that by having a positive outcome to work towards each day it gave me something to look forward to and a reason to keep going. My vision and my dreams were so big that if I didn't persevere it would be a disservice to all of those people that I am meant to serve. I also needed to do this for my children and our future.

3. What did you learn from the experience

I learned that you can achieve your goals no matter what your circumstances are. However, you do need to work on your mindset and vision daily. And to not see failure or rejection as a reason to stop and, instead, see it as a signal to pivot and find another way. The main strategy I used was to ensure that I surrounded myself with like-minded people who were striving for similar things in their life and business. This is really important when trying to do something "different" to the norm. When you set out to work on your own business and work on your passion you will find there will be people who will not understand why you don't just have a "9-5" job! You need to have laser focus and consistency and not let other people's opinions get to you. You have to have a passion and a "why" for doing what you are setting out to do that is bigger than your own personal needs. This is essential in not giving up, you have to have that drive every day that even if you get rejected, ridiculed, or told that you need to do it a different way it doesn't matter you must listen to your gut. If you feel that you should be doing something a certain way, but it is different to others it is important to go with what you want to do. You can still take advice from others but just take the parts that you need.

4. What did you learn about yourself from this experience?

I learned that I was a lot stronger than what I thought. That I could in fact achieve hard things and that some things that I previously would have stressed over no longer were a big issue. My characteristics were built through extremely tough circumstances where I had no choice either to sink or swim. Through my grit, determination and discipline I am creating a life on my terms. My children are my why and my reason for everything. Through my hardships I can now apply this to my business, now I don't get stressed over small things as I know everything can be worked out, strategized over and a successful outcome achieved. I am very savvy with working out solutions and continuing to strive forward in times of adversity. I utilize these tools and skills in every business transaction and coach others through the same methods to empower others through my leadership skills.

5. What do you believe are the most important characteristics and skills one must possess to have a successful life?

The most important characteristics and skills one must possess to have a successful life are resilience, a growth mindset, confidence, consistency and determination. To have resilience you will continue even through the hard times, the times when it all seems too much, too overwhelming, too stressful you will still keep going. A growth mindset will help you see the positives and opportunities in everything you do. Even if it seems like a setback, you will still be able to see the light at the end of the tunnel. In order to have success you must grow; no one becomes successful overnight, it has to be worked for. Having confidence will set you miles apart from everyone else, self-belief and knowing that you can do it is half the battle. Being able to walk into a room or meeting and having the confidence to show up and show others what you can bring to the table will give you the edge you need in business. Consistency is key. If you want to actually achieve, you must take action every single day. Even if you don't feel like it you must do something daily to make progress. Determination and drive will keep you going, you have to want it bad enough, you have to be determined to succeed no matter what. These are the key ingredients to being successful in business and in life. I guarantee with all of this you will achieve your dreams and remember it is not a race it is a journey so embrace it and don't stop.

6. How do you use these skills and characteristics in your home business and for your clients?

Professional development and personal growth are very important to me, from getting my Education degree, teaching students, then teaching at University and adult learning I have always remained a teacher, coach, educator throughout my whole career. Every day I strive to learn, grow and develop. I am a life-long learner and with everything I do in business or life I know that there is a lesson to be learnt. Nothing in life is a failure, it is all an opportunity to learn something new and then grow from it. I am part of many different business groups and attend a variety of conferences and networking events in Australia and overseas throughout the year. I also surround myself with others who are striving towards similar goals and working on similar things. I invest in myself and my team to ensure that we have the most up to date skills and learning so that we can offer the best services and training to our clients.

My business is focused heavily on professional development as we teach and run online programs for businesses to upskill their staff. We are continually updating our skills and up-levelling what we are doing so that our customers are getting the best experience possible. We strive to keep our training internally the most up to date so that we can update and deliver our own content and training with the latest knowledge and information. I also have coaching with my students and run workshops and online conferences on a regular basis.

All skills and strategies that I use to run my business we teach others to utilize also. This helps our clients save time and money and have a strong foundation either in their business or their work.

Our motto is Empower. Grow. Succeed. Inspire through learning.

By: Isla Brook

Isla Brook is a Business Consultant with over 10 years' experience working with some of the world's fastest growing Inc500 businesses, online entrepreneurs and Corporate businesses predominantly in Australia, USA and around the world. She is CEO of Isla Brook Consulting and Founder of The Executive Assistant Academy & The Institute of Professional Development. Isla has experience in running projects, managing and leading teams, teaching professional and personal development workshops, managing projects at an Executive level, managing worldwide global teams. She consults to companies all around the world to help implement strategies and tools into their businesses to save time and money and build strong foundations and systems so that the CEO can move forward as the visionary to keep them driving their business forward.

Isla is a proud mum to two amazing daughters, Lillie and Charlotte. She is very passionate about empowering and giving others the tools and resources to do what she has done, she helps other CEO's recruit and train Executive Assistants and also gives others opportunities to work virtually and become Executive Virtual Assistants through her Executive (Virtual) Assistant Academy. She also provides businesses with high end professional development and leadership training for their teams through The Institute of Professional Development.

By: Isla Brook

www.islabrookconsulting.com
IG: @islabrook
IG: @executiveassistantacademy
IG: @mamas_support_mamas
FB: Executive Assistant Academy
www.evacourse.com

Twitter: Islabrook
LinkedIn: https://www.linkedin.com/in/isla-brook-b96a87178/
Pinterest: https://www.pinterest.ca/executiveassistantacademy/

Scan me

AM I REALLY THE ONE TO DELIVER THE 4 GIFTS?

By: Cheryl Bassitt

There it was, the notice on the front door and big red letters stamped across my brain. After 101 showings with what prospective buyers said was the "wrong" color kitchen cabinets or the "wrong" color of wood, we had to face the reality that our home was going into foreclosure.

If you have ever seen the movie, "The Big Short", it revealed how the financial crisis of 2008 was triggered by the housing bubble. That was us to a "T". Completely upside down in our mortgage, and out of time.

That night we called a family meeting. The boys, both teenagers, sat down at the kitchen table. When I shared the news that we would have to move, they didn't respond by falling apart, ranting or slamming doors. Instead they asked "What do you need us to do?"

For many families this news would have been devastating. The kind of financial struggles that can often tear families apart.

For us, we knew it was time for our "team" to kick it into high gear. With all hands in, we knew our challenge was to navigate through it staying in harmony with one another. I am not going to say it didn't suck... because it did!

However, there was not a single fight, no one pointed fingers, and no one felt sorry for themselves.

I don't share this to boast, but simply to share how we built an unshakeable foundation that stayed firm - even when life got tough.

So, how did we get to a place where no matter what challenges we faced, we knew we would be there for one another? The answer is wrapped in "The 4 Gifts".

These 4 Gifts have been the foundation for my family: how we listen, how we respect, how we show up, how we celebrate our lives.

They have also been my guiding force in business through all the ups and downs. I always say, thank goodness we don't really know how long it might take to see our passions come alive. Otherwise, we might turn and run as fast as possible in the opposite direction!

I still have days where the task to realize my "business" success seems daunting. My most common, recurring roadblock is this thought, "Am I really the one to deliver this message?"

After years of standing on the edge of my mission, I now know that, yes, I am the one. In fact, I am the only one who can deliver the 4 Gifts, because I've lived them. They are my story.

How our journey began...

After spending most of the day trying to figure out how to rob Peter to pay Paul, my sons Brian and David came bounding home from school to announce all the things I needed to buy them. The list ranged from socks to a school t-shirt to baseball cleats and the list seemed never ending.

With my head spinning, I calculated how much we had spent in just a few moments of conversation. Then it happened! Brian asked if I would take him to the store for a tube of Chapstick®. Yes, it was the tiny tube of chapstick that pushed me over the edge and into an emotional meltdown that stopped both boys in their tracks and left them wondering if mom had completely lost her mind.

After I regained my composure, I realized that we all needed to be on the same page. That night, we had our first official family meeting. We also found 3 tubes of Chapstick® and the start of our journey to the 4 Gifts.

The 4 Gifts didn't happen overnight and initially we called them rules, but as our "rules" evolved, so did our meetings. We determined that the word "rules" felt limiting. How we were connecting was anything but limiting! Our connection felt freeing, positive and expanding.

So, every Sunday at 7 pm, we met at the kitchen table and we listened, we laughed, we supported one another - we became a team.

I'll be honest, when we held our first meeting, I was certain I would impart all my wisdom onto my children. I quickly found out that they had a lot to share and I had a lot to learn.

It is this humble attitude that I now take into every meeting no matter how much I think I may know.

I cherish the day I decided to step into a company and share our journey and the 4 Gifts which would later, along with a family meeting toolkit, be awarded one of "The Next Best Brilliant Ideas for Humanity". I did not see that one coming!

THE 4 GIFTS

Gift #1 – The Gift of Listening - "Disconnect to Connect"

TEDX Speaker and author of Start With Why Simon Sinek says, "We are more connected and disconnected than ever before. I have lost count how many times I have witnessed a family out to dinner and every single one of them is on their cell phone or tablet. Not just the kids, I mean everyone!

So, how do we listen, really listen to one another? It starts by putting away the technology - if only for a short while. This does not mean that technology is bad. Like money, technology is energy; it is what we do with it that counts.

However, there needs to be a time and place when the person sitting in front of you is more important than your cell phone, the latest app, or the next viral video. Putting away the technology is great for strengthening family relationships, but it is equally important in business. You honor someone when you give them your "full" attention.

Gift #2 – The Gift of Respect - "Don't Quack the Duck"

If I could have bought a bottle labeled self-esteem, I would have poured it on my kids daily. Life is not about how others see us, but how we see ourselves. When we respect ourselves, we value who we are. I always think of the movie Forest Gump and how Forest's mama gave him an unwavering faith and belief in himself.

As a fun way to evolve our discussions and dig into sharing our ideas, we used a yellow rubber duck sitting on the table during our family meetings. In this scenario, the duck represents an idea. We applied a "no duck-quacking rule" and we were off. If someone had an idea, you could compliment it, build on it, ask questions about it, but you were not immediately allowed to shoot down the duck, or the idea.

This may seem too easy, but what it does is open the door to a whole new conversation and engages a process that fosters creativity and confidence.

Everyone has ideas that deserve to be heard and everyone deserves to feel respected in the process. Does that mean that some ideas might ultimately get tossed out? Sure, but no one should feel like their idea was not worthy enough to discuss.

When we value and respect one another, our words, and our ideas, it feels good. The challenge is, sometimes we don't even realize how quick we are to dismiss ideas, especially our own. I know when I start "quacking", i.e. dismissing my ideas too much, it's because I am doubting myself. When this happens, I put myself in a grown-up time-out to reflect, meditate and find my center again.

I have shared this yellow duck exercise in companies. All I can say, there is a whole lot of quacking going on!

Gift #3 – The Gift of Awareness - "Live Above the Mark"

First, it's important to understand the difference between Living Above the Mark and Living Below the Mark. When you embrace "Above the Mark" living, you take charge of your life, you own your choices, and you believe in your power to change. When you live Below the Mark, you pass blame, you justify your decisions with excuses, and you sit in denial. Living Below the Mark is weighted down in doubt and, often, guilt. Sometimes, we know we are

Below the Mark and choose to stay there. But the first step is to recognize that you cannot make a meaningful change until you are ready to step Above the Mark and own it.

One of the most powerful examples of Living Above the Mark came from my 13-year old son. I was explaining that when we live below the mark, we give our power away to someone or something and that only when we step up above the mark and say "this is my life and I own it", can we start to make a meaningful change. When asked if that made sense, David's response made me realize he understood it beyond measure.

He said, "I totally get it. What you are saying is that last night when we lost our baseball game, we all just sat around blaming the umpire. We never looked at ourselves, so tomorrow night we won't play any better as a team than we did last night."

The good news is, your kids will get this. The bad news is… your kids will get this… and hold you accountable!

I once asked David what he thought would happen if all our leaders in Washington couldn't point fingers and had to live Above the Mark for a whole day. His immediate response was, "I am pretty sure they would have to shut it down." That's a point that is hard to argue with - now more than ever before.

Living Above the Mark and standing in the awareness of when I am choosing not to own my role has been key to moving my business forward. In the "awareness" of where I am, I can choose to stay stuck, or I can choose a different decision.

Gift # 4 – The Gift of Love - "Celebrate Ourselves and Others"

One of our favorite family quotes we shared is, "When you judge someone, you are not defining them, you are defining yourself as someone who is judgmental." We had many deep meaningful discussions around just this one quote.

We talked about how the real beauty in this world is that we are all different. The strength of a team comes from bringing together unique talents, skills and perspectives. The boys could really relate to this concept with sports analogies. I agree with whomever said sports imitate life.

Putting aside our judgment gave us a clearer vision to see the good around us. Obviously, if someone has negative intentions, then there is nothing to celebrate. But when families seek how to support one another, when business teams strive to reach a certain goal, when athletes work in harmony to win, therein lies the beauty. This approach becomes the collective heartbeat and awareness of that which makes us different ultimately comes together to make us strong.

The real celebration begins when you can live in your truth and embrace who you are without judgment or fear. Looking at the world through this lens has allowed me to remove all the drama from my business. When someone does something out of harmony with where I am, I can easily let it go. I don't have to judge it, just trust that it wasn't the right fit.

The Bottom Line:

The Four Gifts created an awareness that weaved into our everyday lives and impacted our relationships with others... our family, our friends, our neighbors, our peers. We embraced these truths as a family and left our kitchen table knowing the following:

- Words matter
- How we treat each other matters
- How we listen to and respect one another matters
- Owning our choices and doing our part matters
- Celebrating ourselves and those around us matters

By incorporating the 4 Gifts into our lives, we learned how to agree to disagree with respect, how to build bridges instead of walls, how to own our choices and consequences, how to listen; really listen, and how to celebrate ourselves and one another.

These 4 Gifts remain our compass, and I employ them every time I sit and connect with someone - whether it's the kitchen table or the boardroom table.

Thank Goodness I didn't know how long it would take!

I didn't know how long it would take to find my voice, how many times I would have to relaunch my business, or how often I would question if I was the one to deliver the 4 Gifts.

What I do know is that I am reminded of how powerful our connection as family was and still is every time I connect with my children. I hear their strength and conviction of what they believe. I witness how they handle life with grace. I see their willingness to communicate and share.

I find my greatest strength in knowing my life's work can be witnessed in how my family and I live our lives. It has everything to do with how I show up in the world... committed in my journey, and the only one who can share this message - perfectly wrapped up in 4 Gifts.

By: Cheryl Bassitt

Inspired by her own family's journey, Cheryl's work for creating unshakable, unbreakable families is recognized as one of the top 5 Next Best Brilliant Ideas for Humanity.

Cheryl is referred to as the common-sense coach, taking a practical approach to life, family values and communication. After two decades as the Executive Director for a major health care association, she then embarked on an entrepreneurial journey that led her back home... literally.

As an author and speaker, she shares that journey and a true pathway of how to connect with your family for life. Her message is grounded in 4 Gifts that foster personal responsibility, effective communication, goal setting, and what it means to truly celebrate ourselves and others.

Her Award-Winning Unstoppable Family Meeting Toolkit, along with the 4 Gifts, gives you everything you need today, to have an unstoppable connection with your family tonight. However, Cheryl's message doesn't stop at the kitchen table...her 4 Gifts are powerful at boardroom tables around the globe. To discover the 4 Gifts and uncover more of Cheryl's work visit www.UnstoppableConnections.com or scan the code below.

By: *Cheryl Bassitt*

www.facebook.com/unstoppableconnections
https://www.linkedin.com/in/cherylbassitt/

Scan me

THE BOOMERANG EFFECT

Dr. Sharon Jones

1. What is the one defining moment during your entrepreneurial journey that transformed and changed the trajectory of your life and/or business?

The ultimate change happened one morning in 2011 when I was passed for a job that I thought I was perfect for on paper but ultimately it was not the right place. I had completed my doctorate and given birth to my first son and I thought my next step was to go to higher education, but fate had other plans. When I applied for the position, I went to the school for a full day interview, guest lectured in a class, and spoke with multiple professors across the school. I remember driving home and thinking what an incredible day and how it felt as though my dreams of becoming a university professor were well on their way of coming true.

The next few weeks were brutal as I waited for the response. Then an email came from the lead professor stating they had chosen another candidate. It was heart wrenching, I felt I had failed as an educator and as a provider for my family. I had a new baby, I was on a third-year teacher pay as a public-school teacher as our salaries had been frozen with the recession, and I was mentally suffering from postpartum. The

After a few days of a lot of crying, I went back to the advice my mom gave me many years ago, give yourself something to look forward to each day.

So in the depths of my sadness, I found something to look forward to each day. Sometimes it was dinner out, or a piece of chocolate in my lunch, a great lesson plan, or the laugh of my newborn son. And slowly, I begin to find myself again.

Then one morning, walking up the steps to my classroom it just hit me, I am going to create my own destiny. There were so many factors that were a part of my world in education but the one factor I knew I could control was me. I have always been an out of the box teacher as teaching computer science is a challenging discipline. So I often brought many different curricula into learning programming as the connections helped the students learn. But on that day in 2012, I realized it was time to take it up to another level and thus my entrepreneurial journey began inside a classroom at Phillip O. Berry Academy of Technology.

I began to reach out to more community members and bring them into my classroom to show how what we were learning was actually being used in the real world and to show the community what we were doing in the school. I shifted my classroom to project-based learning and often flipped the classroom, where students were to listen to the "lecture" at home and then in class we applied. I embraced the notion and applied the work from my adult learning doctoral studies of being a true facilitator to my students and allowing them the opportunity to fail forward and grow. Through applying the adult learning processes, our classroom became a mini experiential lab. Content was relevant, timely, applicable to student interest, and we leveraged storytelling. It was a game changer.

My mindset change opened doors to new opportunities. We were recognized in the community for our collaborations and students were provided experiences pivotal to their education. And for me, the most influential change was when I applied, and I am still one of the original Code.org facilitators. As I mentioned, we were frozen in pay from 2008-2013 and I was at a third-year teacher pay. By 2013, I had married, had my first son, was pregnant with our second, and completed my doctoral degree. My confidence was up in how I could facilitate and we needed a bit more income. So, I read the email that Code.org was looking for facilitators and I applied. Our requirements were three workshops a year and we would receive a stipend. Well those three workshops turned into ten! And my side hustle was alive. The work with

Code.org is the catapult that moved my work of working with teachers and integrating computer science into all disciplines as a side hustle into my full-time business.

I look back on not getting the position at the university and realize it was exactly what was supposed to happen and I found my path as a result.

2. How did you persevere during this moment?

For the first time in my teaching career, I had clarity. I could make change and let my true gifts shine. Being an educator is the most rewarding career but it is often marred by government, testing pressure, and other outside influences but returning

3. What did you learn from the experience?

I learned that once I followed my heart and my gut, that what is meant to be will happen.

4. What did you learn about yourself from this experience?

It has been challenging, overwhelming, rewarding and truly fulfilling. I have always been ambitious but jumping into full time entrepreneurship has been an ambition way out of my comfort zone.

5. What do you believe are the most important characteristics and skills one must possess to have a successful life?

Be true to yourself! I call it the boomerang. What do you always go back too as your passion or your love and natural talent, there you will find your success.

6. How do you use these skills and characteristics in your home business and for your clients?

Working and teaching adults is similar and yet different than working with students. As an adult, our life experiences have more of an influence over our learning but the execution of learning is similar. These are the factors to keep in mind with helping another learn:

- The content presented should have immediate usefulness to the learners.
- The content presented should be relevant to adult learners' lives.

- The training environment should be welcoming so that all learners feel safe to participate.
- Create experiential learning

When I am working with individuals to find their tech genius, I always start with what they enjoy. It is art, numbers, tinkering, logic, etc. Then we dive into how we can make them successful. Finding their own inner talents will help with learning a new skill. We find what is relatable and grow!

Dr. Sharon Jones

Dr. Sharon Jones, Ed.D is the founder and CEO of thedot. Consulting and the Dottie Rose Foundation, where she creates, innovates and implements cutting edge technology focused on new age education. Dr. Jones is a highly sought after and national award winning Computer Science educator in the public school system and for corporate training. Dr. Jones has presented and been published nationally and internationally on data analytics, educational practices and technology. Her book A Recipe for Success Using SAS University: How to Plan Your First Analytics Project is being used in curriculum and classrooms around the country. When not running the technology-world, Dr. Jones spends her time with her husband Ricky, and two sons, Ethan (7) and Dylan (4), and their beloved dog, Cooper (10).

SOMETIMES, LIFE JUST HAPPENS

By: Eileen Galbraith

I'll never forget that date, January 7, 2005. This was a turning point for my life that would send me on a journey I would have never been looking for. Alone, in my apartment, the call came. Hearing the familiar voice sent shivers down my spine. How did he find me, why did he find me? So many questions running through my mind at even just hearing the hello and recognizing the voice.

I responded with a sentence that even shocked the caller. "What the hell do YOU want?" My first instinct was to hang up, end the conversation before it could even begin. but, like most of us, curiosity got the best of me so I continued. The next words were so confusing to me that all I could do was to continue to listen.

Has anyone ever gone through a break-up, that moment in time when you realize, and don't want to, that you will no longer have that special person in your life, that you thought you would spend the rest of your life with? That moment came back in 1999, after a not so pleasant divorce we parted ways and never spoke again, until now.

The caller continued "I just wanted you to know that the IRS is looking for you, we owe back taxes to the tune of $40,000 and I'm not paying it".

My thoughts raced; how can this man continue to hurt me? How did this happen? All the thoughts from the last years of my marriage started racing back. Again I asked myself, all while being silent on the phone, HOW could this happen! Hearing that voice again brought me back "hello?"

"I'm here", I said. I could feel my entire body tensing, I just wanted to scream, I managed to calm myself and listened to the rest of the explanation. Afterward I now faced yet ANOTHER challenge in my life and had no clue as to where to begin.

I am a firm believer that whenever life hands you a challenge, a circumstance, or even a mishap, that you have two choices. One being that you can immerse yourself into self-pity, try to ignore whatever that thing is that is in your way and gently move forward in your life believing that, oh well, this is how it is supposed to be and I have no choice but to accept it.

I prefer the second choice, to figure out what the hell went wrong, research a path to resolve the situation and take MASSIVE ACTION. Which is exactly what I was fiercely determined to do. With a burning desire to prove to myself that THIS was not where I was supposed to be, I immediately began to gather all the facts and pursue a purposeful path that would lead me to my desired outcome. I made a CHOICE.

And so, the journey begins! Still struggling with all of the emotional feelings, after all, I was very angry that this was happening to me, gradually I was able to assess the situation. The major obstacle being that I was informed that I owed $40,000 to the IRS for back taxes, mind you, these were taxes I thought were being paid for the last 6 years of my marriage. Unbeknownst to me, my ex was gambling the money away so nothing was ever sent into the IRS. Not such a great thing to learn after being divorced for 5 years.

Fortunately for me, a very good friend was a CPA After having a discussion I learned that there was a solution to my problem but it would take me to places I could never have imagined! This decision would propel me into a world that I would never have sought out on my own. A little-known fact about me, I love to research and learn new things. While in school I belonged to a club called "The Look it up Club". Of course, most of my research back then was at the library or page turning of the encyclopedia! (can you say pre-internet?)

My challenge now became, do I really want to file a personal bankruptcy to release a debt that I was not only unaware of, but that I was not responsible for? I did my due diligence, researched all my options. Yes, I even spoke with the scary IRS agent in my town, who was actually quite nice and very sympathetic. The unanimous conclusion was to file a chapter 7 bankruptcy. It took me 18 months to arrive at this choice.

Now, here is where the fun begins and my journey into becoming a Business Credit and Finance Coach started. For anyone who has already filed a chapter 7 or 13 Bankruptcy, or even thinking about it, I am here to show you that is does not have to be as traumatic for you as it was for me.

The shame, the stigma and the worry of what others would think of me was overwhelming. I never told anyone in my family what I was doing (I am the youngest of 6), did not seek out any other advice except from my CPA, IRS, and a bankruptcy attorney. I felt embarrassed and humiliated that at this point in my life I had to resort to this endeavor.

Afterall, I was a successful smart woman in my industry, how could I have let this happen to me.?

Sometimes, life just happens. Then, we get to decided how we will receive and handle what has happened. In this, we build our personal character, strength and spirituality. We truly learn what we are made of as a person. It may have taken me years to release the shame but it took me less time to recover from the experience.

Gradually I began to recover from the bankruptcy, and not with the help of the lawyers. You see, as I was going through the process I kept asking "What will this do to my credit and how do I go about restoring it"? They had no answers for me. Thus begins another journey. fAter extensive research I began to understand how this whole credit thing worked. I started to take some steps and documented everything I was doing to improved my credit rating.

Within a year of my bankruptcy being discharged, I put into practice the information and had great success. Finally, I was able to share my experience with a friend who asked me to help them.

This was easier now because I was documenting all of the steps that I took, eliminated the ones that were not effective and fine-tuned those that were. With another success behind me, I spoke with another friend. And on and on until I now had a deliverable way to assist those in need of such a service. I began to teach others how to improve their credit profiles and soon, a business started to form.

Knowledge is more important to me than just having someone else do all the work for me. I continued with this value while working with many more people over the years. Sure, it is important to make sure your credit profiles are accurate, but the real value comes in understanding the elements of a personal credit score and how to maintain that score, long after I am gone. There are so many things that your personal credit scores are used for, having this information improves your chances of getting the best value for your money.

It was never my intent to start down this path of entrepreneurship, my awareness became more significant as more and more people believed in me and what I had to offer. As I surrounded myself with a supportive group, hired mentors and coaches along the way, I realized the impact I could have for business owners and continued to grow and expand my business to include Business Credit and Financing options.

Was this an easy journey? Absolutely not! Did I know what I was getting into? Do any of us? There were many uphill climbs to experience and I must tell you, for every backward slide down that hill, it was so much more rewarding while climbing back up.

I started this all while still working a full-time job. And, that is exactly what I would recommend to anyone looking to start their own business. There are so many things to learn along the way and keeping that security of a monthly pay check, well, sometimes we may need that.

Entrepreneurship can be a very lonely path, I work from an office in my home, sometimes this feels isolated. Fortunately, as a Speaker, I travel often so I am among those entrepreneurs that continue to lift my spirits. Surrounding yourself with those positive souls who "get you" is very rewarding.

Never underestimate the power of connections. People will astound and surprise you when you see what we are all capable of, live in your spotlight and allow others in so they too can shine brightly. Isolation is not conducive to impacting the world around you, only when we allow ourselves to step into our truly unique greatness can we inspire others.

In the beginning, I did isolate myself, my clients' work can easily be completed on my computer. I didn't need to travel, or so I thought. It wasn't until I clearly made the decision to get in front of as many people as I could, because my passion is to serve those entrepreneurs seeking funding so that they too can grow their business and get their genius out into the world, that I began to realize the amount of people I could help.

Speaking, for me, was not something I would have sought out to do. Isn't it amazing that when you make a decision to do something and begin to act on it that the Universe conspires to help? That is exactly what occurred for me and my business. Get over the fear and great things happen. People that I would never have made connections with started to appear. I am truly blessed with those that are in my inner circles now and all of the inspiring, heart centered Entrepreneurs I have had the privilege to meet and call friends.

Hopefully what you have read so far will create a spark inside of you. It is my wish that this will inspire you to take action. Not just any action, Bold action. Honestly, there have been many times where I was ready to give up. Yes, I said it. Things felt like they were too hard or too complicated to do, I stressed after finally leaving my secure job as to where the monthly income was going to come from. I stressed, I panicked, I tried talking myself into quitting! Yet, each and every time I pressed forward, I reached out for help and support and received it graciously.

Today, I am extremely grateful that I kept moving forward, one day at a time one client at a time. Gradually the momentum that I longed for began to show up. This happened for several reasons. First, I became very clear on who I served and how I served them. Second, I made the commitment to be the best for my clients and to truly be at my very best. Third, I hired a mentor, several in fact. These are the people who believe in me, see my dreams and goals and walk this path with me.

Before I end, I want to recognize the most important person in my life, John, my Business Partner and Life Partner. Without him, none of this would have been possible. His belief in my determination to make this work, as a business, has been a driving force for us. For that, I am truly blessed and loved.

By: Eileen Galbraith

Eileen E Galbraith is Co-Owner of Credit Knowhow, LLC. Located in Havertown, PA

As a Business Credit and Finance Coach, Entrepreneurs, such as those reading this, hire me to help you get the money you need to start, grow or scale your business. While working with my clients we formulate a business credit plan that builds the foundation for establishing credit in the name of the business, which positions the business to access more financial opportunities and frees them

from using their personal credit to invest in their business. This removes risk and liability from the personal family and places it directly onto the business, thereby protecting your assets.

With a 10-year history working within the field of Credit, Eileen's insights, knowledge and strategic thinking processes bring outstanding results for her clients. Whether you are seeking to analyze your Personal Credit to improve your scores or you desire to begin to build Credit in the name of the Business, or you are seeking capital (funding) opportunities, we have a solution for you.

Keeping your credit safe, both Personal and Business is easy with our Identity Theft Protection Process.

To learn how to begin to build credit in the name of your business, download this FREE E-Book

www.TheCreditGal.biz/OBC

Scan me

LA RAISON D'ÊTRE: OVER 50 AND NEVER TOO LATE

By: Jean-Michel Tournier

In the 21st century perhaps you, like me, have been given a second chance to design a new life and become the person you were meant to be. This is not the way it was back in my Father's Day.

In the 20th century, men like my father — who worked as a patent engineer in the automobile industry all his life — rarely changed careers. However, with the advent of technology, reinventing yourself is today's new norm. Even so, changing careers can seem risky, especially after age 50, when it looks like you're throwing away a lifetime of experience.

Then again, sometimes reinventing yourself is choiceless; life hands it to you unsolicited and unexpectedly. French by birth, historically three generations of my family called Algeria home. As French nationals they became known as 'pieds-noirs' — slang for the European immigrants who settled Algeria mid-19th century.

During the Algerian War of Independence, the French were targeted for assassination. It was loyal Algerians working on the farms managed by my grandparents who sent advance warnings safeguarding their survival. In 1962, the pieds-noirs were given two choices: "la valise ou le cercueil" (the suitcase or the coffin). Limited to two suitcases, families abandoned their farms and houses, their cars and household belongings. Repatriated to France, they found their 'patrie' less than welcoming. Exiled from their beloved Algeria, my family was forced to reinvent themselves in a country that did not know them or care about them.

You could say my family has the engineering gene in its DNA! My dad's sisters were the first female engineers to work on the French Phénix and Super-Phénix nuclear reactors. Dad's brother is a world-renowned hydroelectric power plant and dam civil engineer.

My mom dreamed of being a teacher. She loved math and although it was an unacceptable choice for girls back then, she chose to follow her heart and the advice of her father, "Jo, trust me. It's a lot easier to grade a math problem than a philosophy paper."

She earned her Bachelor's at age 15 in Algeria from an all-boys Lycée (school). Studying in France next, she was the only girl to graduate from Aix-en-Provence Université in a male dominated curriculum, and younger than most.

True to her calling, she became an educator and taught mathematics in the Lycée system. She also tutored students in need of mastering math concepts. I inherited my family's love affair with math along with my mother's dream of teaching as well as her dedication and caring for students.

At 21, I was improving car engine combustion models on Cray super-computers, and developing my own Chess playing program. Following in my father's footsteps, I graduated from École Centrale de Paris, the most prestigious Professional Engineering School in France. I didn't know it at the time, but my software engineering and computer science skills would become the backbone of my consulting business nearly 25 years later.

However, back in my teens, I discovered being a nerd was not top-of-mind with girls. Never considered dating material, I was chased after only for my tutoring skills. Thirty years later, things have changed. Technology is in and so are the geeks! Geekishness — the new cool — is now next to godliness.

"Everyday magic connecting us to the Divine is present for all of us. Although it comes and goes as quickly as it appears. Darting and weaving through our lives unpredictably. Extraordinarily. Inexplicably. Mysteriously. Unexpectedly. "
– Pamela McDonough

I believe there is magic making in our everyday lives. I believe unseen forces are always at work for our benefit; creating life-changing connections to people, places and things. To see it, we need only to watch.

While working at the French Energy Atomic Commission in Saclay, I had a powerful and vivid dream. It held the promise of righting the wrong of a love lost — one long since mired in antiquity.

In the dream, I remember being on a quest to find my soulmate, but the search was in vain. Not finding her, I knew with certainty that she lived in a faraway place and if we were to be together, I had to leave France.

Was it a dream or a calling? There was a sense of urgency about it. Like a calling, it consumed my every thought. At the time, I did not know that a calling chooses you. And that commitment required leaps of faith and hope, and trials of risk and uncertainty.

Whatever the reason for the dream, pursuing it meant leaving my close-knit family along with the promise of a career with the CEA. Mysteriously, just a few days prior to my dream, I was offered the opportunity to earn a Ph.D. at the University of New Mexico, USA.

There's no denying the hand of heaven that brought me to Albuquerque — carrying only one indestructible blue Samsonite suitcase — had also arranged a chanced meeting 10 years later with a special woman. There was magic in the déjà vu moment on the ballroom dance floor when I knew, without a doubt, my dance partner was the woman from my dream.

After completing my Ph.D. in aerospace and nuclear engineering at UNM, I held a Research Professorship for nearly 20 years. As a senior research scientist and principal co-investigator with the Institute for Space and Nuclear Power Studies, I was responsible for highly complex and collaborative studies with universities, national laboratories and aerospace agencies: from designing spacecraft to send astronauts to Mars and Jupiter, to developing nuclear power plants for desalination and the hydrogen economy; all opportunities to leverage my software engineering and problem-solving skills while performing breakthrough research.

During my tenure at UNM, teaching graduate level classes to onsite students and offsite engineers from the Los Alamos and Sandia National Laboratories was the fortuitous happenstance through which I discovered my passion and talent for mentoring and coaching.

For a time, academia paved the way for my long-held dream of making a difference in the world of science, and in the lives of aspiring engineers who came knocking on my door. They found it always open and they came to appreciate my availability and guidance in their Master's and Ph.D. research projects and coursework.

By that time, I had over 150 publications under my belt, earning international recognition in the engineering community. Despite my success, something kept nagging at the corners of my mind. Eventually, I came to realize that I had lost my passion for academia. I felt stuck, unmotivated and wanting to move on. But where? And how?

In 2012, a series of events unfolded that changed my life forever. It began with the 'sound of distant drums' and increased US military operations in the Middle-East. During wartime, military budgetary requirements cut across the board. It was felt dramatically at UNM when government funded research dried up. At the same time, our engineering department was tasked with mandatory reorganization and inevitable personnel cutbacks. I was two years away from retirement and went from being a rocket scientist to: "What am I going to do for the rest of my life?"

To complicate matters, while I had been engaged in designing craft for outer space travel, the job market had become saturated with young newcomers. Things had changed dramatically. As a Ph.D., I was labeled overqualified. Nearing 50, my potential for ready employment was highly unlikely.

> *" Put your heart, mind and soul into even your smallest acts.*
> *This is the secret to success. "*
> *– Master Swami Sivananda*

It was about the same time that a long-time consulting client and friend, seeking to expand his sales territory and open a new region, suggested a partnership. His vision included my receiving a substantial initial salary building and managing a portable building manufacturing plant in Arizona. He knew I had no hands-on experience in assembly and fabrication, but he thought my engineering background would be an asset.

I was excited by this opportunity to develop new skills. However, my years in academia, French background and strong work ethic did not prepare me for the reality of an unmotivated work force on welfare, rampant drug usage and addiction, and frequent theft. On more than one occasion, police arrived to investigate reported gunshots or perform drug busts.

Watching these men's lives spiral out of control was heartbreaking. I know you can't help everyone, but I never missed an opportunity to say an encouraging word or extend kindness or a helping hand. Yet, nothing I said or did mattered. Their hearts just weren't into making any changes.

Eighty-to-ninety hours was my standard work week from day one. While the operation generated millions of dollars for the bankers/investors, being tight fisted with the budget made little difference in a culture where sales and production, hampered by the intense Arizona heat and the yo-yoing nature of the two-season market (hot and hotter), merely covered cost of goods, services, equipment and labor. As plant manager, coming away empty handed on pay day became too often the norm.

Nearly 3 years into it, the plant and its burdens hung around my neck like Coleridge's albatross. Although we worked shoulder-to-shoulder, the men cared little for my altruistic behavior. And, there was no denying the line they had drawn in the Arizona sand, or that I stood alone on the opposite side. A hostile takeover from a trusted foreman was the final coup de grâce. As signer or co-signer for the business loans and plant assets, I was forced into bankruptcy.

> *"Sometimes, our most challenging relationships bring the greatest personal blessings. "*
> *– Doreen Virtue*

In retrospect, this tremendous loss was a blessing in disguise, which in turn propelled me into the next phase of my career. It took dogged determination on a day-to-day basis to make the manufacturing operation work against all odds. I realized then that if I could do that, I could accomplish anything I put my mind to.

And as it turned out, my personal experience with age discrimination helped me relate to my clients. Here was the Universe at work; turning ageism into a blessing to help me understand what a career transition felt like on a personal and emotional basis.

There's more. I have been blessed with a thirst for knowledge and am accustomed to delving into complex concepts on my own. One of my favorite science fiction writers, Isaac Asimov considered being self-taught the gold standard: "Self-education is, I firmly believe, the only kind of education there is."

In my experience, self-education is akin to everyday miracles. Like any other life experience, it takes time, energy and persistence, but at the end of the day, 'voila' you have the makings of great happenings.

Another everyday miracle came about when I set my intention to self-educate and familiarize myself with web technology and its intricacies. Doing so enabled me to introduce unique SEO, branding and marketing strategies and solutions which benefit my clients and their businesses.

My beautiful wife (yes, the woman of my youthful dream and my soulmate) tells me that I am blessed with the ability to roll with change, engage the unknown with boldness, and hold steady; that we nurture our future into fruition with every word and deed.

> *" No star is ever lost we once have seen, we always may*
> *be what we might have been."*
> *– Adelaide Anne Procter*

My affinity with math and strategic thinking is an advantage in today's tech-savvy environment. And although technological innovations expedite results, the requisite element when unlocking a person's potential is essentially the human touch.

Research indicates that more than 70% of Americans are unhappy and feel stuck in an uninspiring career. They haven't figured out what they love doing and lack 'Ikigai' (the reason for which you wake up in the morning) or 'Raison d'Être' (reason for being).

The ancient Greeks considered happiness to be: "the joy you feel striving toward your potential." Our whole life changes when we use our particular gifts and talents to do something we love. Taking the risk brings about happiness and fulfillment — our 'Raison d'Être'. Making a difference in a meaningful way is the reason we get up happier in the morning and look forward to the day.

I enjoy helping clients contemplating a second-act career tap into their innate abilities. To make them stand out in today's competitive marketplace and connect quickly with decision-makers requires branding, SEO and web technology.

The icing on the cake, or 'cerise du gâteau' as we say in France, is LinkedIn; technology's gift of global networking. It's the ultimate helpmate for mid-lifers seeking a new career or setting in motion a successful consulting business.

The motivation for launching 'Spotlighting You' is my first love — the human connection — teaching, coaching and mentoring. This is who I am. It is my calling. It took a dream and a transatlantic move to make it come about.

Making a difference in someone's life, career or business is my reason for being, and I feel blessed every day for the opportunity to do so. As a coach, I assure my clients that there is life after 50 and just because they're a mid-lifer, 'it ain't over 'til it's over'.

By: Jean-Michel Tournier

Jean-Michel was born near Paris, France. A gifted mathematician and engineer, he graduated first of class with a Master's degree in Applied Mathematics and Computer Sciences. He received his Professional Engineering degree from the prestigious École Centrale de Paris.

At age 24, inspired by a powerful dream, he came to America in search of his soulmate and to pursue a doctoral degree in aerospace and nuclear engineering.

Jean-Michel is an internationally recognized scientific author with over 150 publications. As a University Professor, he worked closely with NASA and national laboratories designing spacecraft in response to President Reagan's 'Star Wars' initiative.

In 2015, he melded online branding, SEO web technology and software engineering with coaching, his first love, and founded 'Spotlighting You on the Web'. He is passionate about empowering job hunters and business owners with the knowledge, technology and social media selling skills required to be successful in today's competitive business environment.

He has helped hundreds of clients land their dream job quickly or jump-start and grow successful businesses using his breakthrough LinkedIn branding and marketing strategies system: "Breaking the ICE!" designed to Impress, Connect and Engage.

His clients affectionately call him *"The LinkedIn Rocket Scientist."*

By: Jean-Michel Tournier

His clients affectionately call him "The LinkedIn Rocket Scientist."

Social media links:

LinkedIn: https://www.linkedin.com/in/jmtournier

Facebook: https://www.facebook.com/spotlightingyou/

Twitter: https://twitter.com/spotlightingyou

Scan me

FINDING PURPOSE THROUGH CONNECTION & HELPING OTHERS

By: Miranda DeHaan

One of the beautiful things about entrepreneurship is seeing just how 'on purpose' you've been since the very beginning. My journey into starting Petwell Navigation began when I was about 8 years old, but I didn't realize it until just recently. Like many children, I grew up with parents who did not have a happy relationship. Unresolved conflict surrounded all of us, eventually compelling my parents to separate and get divorced when I was about 5 years old.

I spent many weekends with my dad until his job moved him away from where I lived; then he flew me out to spend summers with him. It was difficult not seeing him for months on end. My mother seemed to struggle with her own emotions, let alone trying to cope and support me as I attempted to adjust without a stable father figure.

As a child, I didn't know how to process my emotions and didn't feel I had the support of anyone who could tell me things like 'it wasn't my fault'. I bottled up my emotions, but emotions eventually come out sideways when buried and not healed and for me, they came out in the form of asthma. I spent a lot of time in hospitals. It seemed that I only had asthma attacks when there was some kind of emotional upheaval in my life, even if it was just getting into trouble for something. I grew up as an only child and often felt very lonely. I was also shy and didn't have many friends, so I spent a lot of time by myself. My mom decided to let me have a kitten when I was around eight years old despite the fact that I was supposed to be allergic and that animals are supposed to be triggers for asthma. Maybe she had some kind of inner knowing that a kitty would be beneficial for me. I decided to name my kitten, Miss Piggy, and she became my rock and my best friend. I don't remember what I told her, but I know I could tell her anything I wanted without being judged and receive complete unconditional love and acceptance. I believe she helped me to cope.

I had some varying experiences with animals throughout the years. When I was around 13 years old, I started volunteering with Little Bits Riding Club which is a therapeutic program for children and adults with physical and mental challenges. My role was to help groom the horses and help lead them around the arena. I volunteered at a few veterinary clinics and was able to learn about the health care side of animals. I also gained experience with reptiles and I learned about them through a club that I was a member of, as well as the opportunity to help educate about wildlife through the Wildlife Rehabilitation Society.

My relationship with Pigpen (aka Miss Piggy), as she came to be known, plus working with other animals ignited my desire to become a veterinarian, though being in the hospital frequently also ignited my desire to become a nurse. I guess, ultimately, I wanted to do something that would help others who were not able to help themselves. I did not end up in either profession, however, but instead ended up taking the Animal Health Technology program at NAIT which, I feel, combines both of those professions. As part of my training in the field, I was required to spend some time in the Euthanasia section of the Edmonton Humane Society. It broke my heart to have to kill these cats, dogs, and other surrendered animals who weren't necessarily sick. Upon reading some of the reasons that pets had been surrendered to the humane society, I realized that if the guardians of these pets had had better access to certain information and resources about pet care, health, and wellness, they may not have felt the need to give up their beloved pets. I discovered while working in the clinics that what I enjoyed the most was helping clients to understand how to care for their pets, whether it be about giving medication, post-operative care, nutrition, or something else.

Later on, after being laid off from the clinic where I was working, I began a pet-sitting business and discovered that though my clients loved their pets and wanted the best for them, they were often lacking information to make the best decisions about their care. I aimed to increase my clients' knowledge and awareness as I went along, but due to financial circumstances, I eventually had to close my business.

I went back to working in the corporate world for a while, but the idea of teaching still percolated in the very back of my mind for the next few years. In reality, I think I was too scared to try a business again and felt more secure with a regular paycheque, so I didn't allow the idea to come to the forefront. The last job I had ended up being very toxic. Most management wasn't willing to hear what I had to say or have any discussions. They liked telling me how to do my job even though they really had no idea what my job entailed. They didn't appreciate or accept my differences. I really wanted to leave, but I waited too long and my energy was already spent. I didn't have the energy to look for jobs, create a new resume and cover letter for each one I wanted to apply for, and then potentially go for interviews. It took all of my energy to get up, go to work, get through the day, and then eventually go home feeling drained only to do it again for another four days. The weekend was not enough time to recover. I eventually found out I was dealing with adrenal fatigue. It took being laid off again, a lack of desire to get another 'job' just to pay the bills, my other earlier experiences with teaching, and a gentle push from someone I was connected with to take the entrepreneur program offered through the government before that idea came to the surface again. I wondered if I could make that my sole focus for a business.

I struggled with a lot of self-doubt and worthiness issues that developed from my childhood experiences, as well as the toxic environments I had spent time in, and spent a lot of time listening to how others thought I should operate my business and how I should behave. Many of these suggestions didn't feel right to me, though I realize the advice I received was well-intentioned. One example of this was when I was told that if I was going into a business social situation, I should act as though I felt fantastic and life was grand to 'create' a more positive vibe even if I was feeling the self-doubt & 'I'm not enough' issues. I could have avoided going to these events, but since this was a frequent feeling in the beginning, it would have meant never going to them. I've never been much of an actor, so the best I could do was smile and say I was ok. I think people can tell when a person is not being authentic, maybe not on a conscious level, but at least on an energetic level. I felt that the people offering me advice knew better than I did what I should do because they were more 'experienced'. But I also ended up with a lot of mixed messages that left me feeling confused. I didn't know what I was supposed to do and I was getting more and more anxious which was freezing me into not taking any action at all. I was frequently feeling like I made a mistake and was not on the path I was meant to be on and kept thinking that maybe I 'should' just go back and look for a 'job'. It wouldn't satisfy me or make me happy, but at least I would know what to expect. There would be familiarity.

I had/have some emotional things going on in my personal life, as well. But, as I've discovered, there really isn't much separation between our business and personal lives and they bleed into one another. I learned from messages that I was given when I was growing up, either verbally or by observation, to do what other people wanted me to do, to make them happy and proud of me, or to at least avoid doing anything that would make me stand out. These messages often came from many authority-type figures. These messages are also very much a part of the corporate world. Much of the management that exists in corporate companies is still a form of dictatorship rather than actual leadership and doesn't tend to invite communication or discussion. Often the underlying threat is that if you try to have a mind of your own, you risk being fired and not having opportunities to advance. I have been a people pleaser all my life and have been afraid to be a unicorn (aka be different), to risk making some people unhappy, and to stand up for my own personal values.

I've always been interested in personal development. Early on in my life, I believe I did things on a subconscious level to challenge myself so that I could grow as a person, but I started to consciously and actively pursue personal growth in my early 30's. Everything I have done prior to me starting this business has been valuable, but has felt very minor in comparison to my experiences now. I believe starting a business is the ultimate in self-growth, if you allow it to be. I took my learnings from being in business before and decided I needed to learn how to build meaningful relationships with other entrepreneurs, learn to communicate as clearly as I can, learn to be authentic, and offer as much value as I can. These decisions have made a huge difference in where I am now with my business and my connection with it. I am also learning how to be vulnerable and visible which are both quite challenging, but I believe are necessary to becoming authentic, to connect with other like-minded individuals, and to find my tribe. To me, being vulnerable is letting people see me as I truly am in my feelings, my values, my beliefs, my mistakes, and also taking actions where there is a risk of rejection. And being visible means standing up for and stating my beliefs and values with the risk of being judged, including showing my vulnerability.

I've discovered that networking is really important in business, but not just networking with anyone in any situation. I have tried various networking and social events, but ultimately, I gravitate to groups where I feel people genuinely want to connect and not just simply pitch their business. I have since found business groups that I can be a part of that value authenticity and offer support to each other when we are struggling. It is through my connections, the relationships that I am building, and sometimes through simple observation that I have begun to feel confidence in myself and in my business.

Talking with other entrepreneurs who are willing to admit their own doubts, fears, and insecurities, I have learned that these concerns/beliefs never completely go away just because we've gained experience. There are hills and valleys throughout the journey and I believe there are layers of our feelings, as well. We push through the doubt, fears, and insecurities in one aspect of business, but face them again when we pursue another area that we are inexperienced with.

My experiences so far have shown me that creating a business or being an entrepreneur isn't something to conquer, that after a certain period of time you'll have it all figured out. It is a continual experience of learning and growing and changing. But that is what life is all about! If we don't have something in our life to challenge us, to push us, to encourage us to grow, then we stagnate and start to feel like we don't have any purpose.

My suggestion, if you decide to take it, is to continually find ways to challenge yourself and get out of your comfort zone. Even if you start to feel stuck or frozen, try to find one small action towards something you want to do. Our comfort zone is like an elastic band. Every time it gets stretched; it never goes back to exactly the same size.

By: Miranda DeHaan

Miranda is an Animal Health Technologist, speaker, teacher, and Chief Navigator of Petwell Navigation. She has been an Animal Health Technologist since 2000 and is a member of ABVMA and ABVTA. Her mission is to help reduce the number of animals ending up in rescue shelters or abandoned and enhance knowledge and awareness.

Miranda created Petwell Navigation out of a desire to help pet guardians navigate and understand information about pet health and wellness because much of it can be misleading, inaccurate, or all-together incorrect and she stays informed and up-to-date through regular continuing education. Through educational talks, workshops, and consultations, she helps guardians feel empowered to make informed decisions so that their pets can be the happiest, healthiest versions of themselves. Miranda also helps to reduce the emotional confusion a person can feel after receiving a diagnosis/treatment from their veterinarian by providing clarity and assistance in asking the necessary questions of their veterinarian before making any decisions.

Miranda is a self-described personal development junkie and aims to always learn from her experiences (intentional & unintentional).

Miranda can be found at:

https://www.facebook.com/petwellnavigationYEG/
https://www.linkedin.com/in/miranda-d-53699a6/
miranda.dehaan@gmail.com

Scan me

TURN YOUR CLIENTS INTO YOUR CHEERLEADERS

By: *Sharon Galluzzo*

1. What is the one defining moment during your entrepreneurial journey that transformed and changed the trajectory of your life and/or business?

I'll never forget the moment when I logged into our business bank account to find that our funds had dwindled down to just $2000. Which, to be honest, is just a one week away from being bankrupt. I couldn't breathe, it felt like I was in a vacuum - all the sound in the room had been sucked out; it was unnaturally silent. I was suspended in that moment as time stopped for what seemed like hours. While my fingers remained on the keyboard, I felt nothing. My mouth was dry. I didn't know whether to panic, cry or get angry and I knew that I was terrified. My brain screamed, "How did I get here?"

I grew up the youngest of five in south-central Pennsylvania. I was a tomboy, spending long summers running around barefoot, climbing trees, dashing through pastures (careful to avoid cow patties) and riding my beloved red tricycle. I had *way* too much energy for our little 3-bedroom, *upstairs* apartment and my awkward phase lasted all the way through high school as I had yet to grow into my features or my personality.

At my earliest opportunity, which happened to be college, I ran off to New York to be an actress. While I decided Broadway was not for me, a cute Italian boy was. Our story began in New York as a married couple until we added our spunky first-born daughter. Changes soon began as we decided to dive head-first into our next experience – moving to the South. We landed in North Carolina and soon added another adorable little girl to our crew.

We did the usual 2-career household shtick until finances forced us to agree that, with two girls in daycare, my job was actually costing us money. I tried to be a stay-at-home housewife, I really did. But my energy and restlessness soon led to direct sales companies and part-time jobs. One day my husband came to me and said, "I want to start a business. I want to be my own boss."

Ever the supportive spouse and adventure junkie I said, "yes." So off we went into the world of business ownership. It was an exciting, heady time. We had big dreams and elaborate plans. We knew exactly how we were going to make our fortune with all the big-paying clients. It was all so exciting and wonderful, until it wasn't.

Until the day the numbers in my bank account predicted my future.

How would we be able to keep the house, much less the business? What would this mean for our young daughters? We had invested so much. I was ashamed and worried... and I was terrified.

2. How did you persevere during this moment?

It honestly took awhile to process all the crazy emotions, but time wasn't our friend. We had to move and move fast. Sometimes lack of time to over think about things is a blessing. It was clear was that we were at a crossroads. We had a decision to make. Either we quit now or figure a way forward. We decided to forge ahead. We decided and then took action – that was the secret sauce. We also fixed our mindset on success.

We refused to let the bank account predict our future. The most important space in any business is the space between your ears. We decided not to give up and not to fail. We agreed that we were going to make this work.

We doubled down on our work ethic. We sought out experts who had succeeded and modeled them. We hired experts to help us fill in the missing pieces.

The path we forged led us to a business making multiple 6-figures year after year, winning industry and community awards and being a leader in our community. We created an atmosphere so attractive to our customers that we had an endless pipeline of referrals. We put it all together. We developed the system.

3. What did you learn from the experience?

What I learned was so simple -- yet so powerful. You see, what I realized was that systems equal freedom.

Have you ever wondered what it would be like to have more clients than you can handle? Have you ever wondered what it would be like to have clients that you love to work with? Have you ever wondered what it would be like to be so profitable and hands free that you can travel the world and live the lifestyle you and your family deserve?

It sounds amazing, right? That is exactly what we figured out.

The very system we built for ourselves, that allowed us to profit in our business, serve our customers and community, be there for our kids and travel, and that I now share with our clients, is used every day in our own business. It includes: the Endless Referral Roadmap System. This is what we do, we create a Roadmap to turn our dream clients into an army sending endless referrals to us.

We found that we needed a system that turned our clients into our cheerleaders, because systems equal freedom.

4. What did you learn about yourself from this experience?

I learned how communication really works and what "they" never told me about business development so we could scale up without burning out. We dug deep behind the curtain to figure out how simple growing our business really was.

I learned that my mission was not just to succeed in my business but to re-ignite the passion other business owners have for their clients and their businesses so that they can enjoy life again.

I love to work with people who are ready to take control of their businesses. People who are set to take the next step into the life they've always deserved -- Entrepreneurs who are ready for transformation.

5. What do you believe are the most important characteristics and skills one must possess to have a successful life?

You must be willing to set aside your own self doubt and just decide to get started. This is a decision point in your life. You need to step up and operate your mind at the level that deserves the high income and success.

That means turn off the voice that says, "I don't think I can do it". Nobody ever thinks they can do it when they get started. I had my doubts! But everything worked out okay. So you're going to be okay too.

Is this making sense?

Does this describe you?

And would this work for you? Of course it will!

Great, because here's the problem... Have you ever considered, that we just don't have all the communication skills that we need. And it's not our fault! They didn't give us a client manual when we started our businesses and there's not enough time to stop everything and get an MA in psychology to figure out what's in our clients' heads and how to communicate so that they can hear us.

Please know my intention is to help you fix that problem, because the more you listen, the more you will learn because the fact that you are reading this means that you are going to make a shift today. Because you are ready to take action now.

6. How do you use these skills and characteristics in your home business and for your clients?

My clients are not people who want to do it the long, hard way. They are not people who are not helping people, I only work with world-changers. And they are not people who are looking for a "get rich quick scheme;" who believe that money is magically deposited into their bank account.

I look for people who are ready to take action and get results now! They've got to be willing to use the system (because systems equal freedom); and I know they will.

They come to me because they're ready for results. They're ready to take action. You see, I can put this "done for you system" in your hands but you've got to use it!

And they must be willing to set aside their own self doubt and just decide to get started. Just like we did. And just like for us, this is a decision point in life. I ask my clients to step up and operate their minds at the level that deserves high income and success.

Imagine and picture this: would you love to be an acknowledged leader in your industry; continually getting referrals from raving clients?

How would it feel to have more quality time with your loved ones because your systems are running smoothly without you?

What if you could help more people, generating endless referrals? That is the exact system we used to generate breakthrough results for ourselves and others.

This is the very system we built for ourselves and our clients use every day in their own businesses. Here is what it includes: The Endless Referral Roadmap System where we create a roadmap to turn your dream clients into an army sending endless referrals for you.

Remember, you need a system that turns your clients into your cheerleaders.

So first, we make your Endless Referral Roadmap for you so that all the essential elements are there and you can't mess it up. We take the guesswork out of the magic by handling it for you. All you have to do is follow the steps.

We'll even tell you the one thing to never do when getting referrals and the sexy Jedi trick to maximizing referrals. We have the proven roadmap and we customize it for you.

Because you are reading this book, because you are an action-taker doing the work and because I want to invest in you. I'm offering readers of Light At the End of The Funnel a way to get this roadmap for free.

Sharon Galluzzo combines practical experience with relatable solutions to increase sales as much as 30% per quarter.

Sharon has been an entrepreneur for more than 18 years. She built a business to $300,000 a year, year after year before selling it to semi-retire. She is a speaker and author who has won over 18 awards for business development.

She specializes in helping entrepreneurs grow their businesses sustainability without killing themselves.

5. What do you believe are the most important characteristics and skills one must possess to have a successful life?

You must be willing to set aside your own self doubt and just decide to get started. This is a decision point in your life. You need to step up and operate your mind at the level that deserves the high income and success.

That means turn off the voice that says, "I don't think I can do it". Nobody ever thinks they can do it when they get started. I had my doubts! But everything worked out okay. So you're going to be okay too.

Is this making sense?

Does this describe you?

And would this work for you? Of course it will!

Great, because here's the problem... Have you ever considered, that we just don't have all the communication skills that we need. And it's not our fault! They didn't give us a client manual when we started our businesses and there's not enough time to stop everything and get an MA in psychology to figure out what's in our clients' heads and how to communicate so that they can hear us.

Please know my intention is to help you fix that problem, because the more you listen, the more you will learn because the fact that you are reading this means that you are going to make a shift today. Because you are ready to take action now.

6. How do you use these skills and characteristics in your home business and for your clients?

My clients are not people who want to do it the long, hard way. They are not people who are not helping people, I only work with world-changers. And they are not people who are looking for a "get rich quick scheme;" who believe that money is magically deposited into their bank account.

I look for people who are ready to take action and get results now! They've got to be willing to use the system (because systems equal freedom); and I know they will.

They come to me because they're ready for results. They're ready to take action. You see, I can put this "done for you system" in your hands but you've got to use it!

And they must be willing to set aside their own self doubt and just decide to get started. Just like we did. And just like for us, this is a decision point in life. I ask my clients to step up and operate their minds at the level that deserves high income and success.

Imagine and picture this: would you love to be an acknowledged leader in your industry; continually getting referrals from raving clients?

How would it feel to have more quality time with your loved ones because your systems are running smoothly without you?

What if you could help more people, generating endless referrals? That is the exact system we used to generate breakthrough results for ourselves and others.

This is the very system we built for ourselves and our clients use every day in their own businesses. Here is what it includes: The Endless Referral Roadmap System where we create a roadmap to turn your dream clients into an army sending endless referrals for you.

Remember, you need a system that turns your clients into your cheerleaders.

So first, we make your Endless Referral Roadmap for you so that all the essential elements are there and you can't mess it up. We take the guesswork out of the magic by handling it for you. All you have to do is follow the steps.

We'll even tell you the one thing to never do when getting referrals and the sexy Jedi trick to maximizing referrals. We have the proven roadmap and we customize it for you.

Because you are reading this book, because you are an action-taker doing the work and because I want to invest in you. I'm offering readers of Light At the End of The Funnel a way to get this roadmap for free.

By: Sharon Galluzzo

S haron Galluzzo combines practical experience with relatable solutions to increase sales as much as 30% per quarter.

Sharon has been an entrepreneur for more than 18 years. She built a business to $300,000 a year, year after year before selling it to semi-retire. She is a speaker and author who has won over 18 awards for business development.

She specializes in helping entrepreneurs grow their businesses sustainability without killing themselves.

What sets Sharon apart is her proven business success, down-to-earth methodologies coupled with an enthusiastic communication style. Hers is not head-knowledge, but in the trenches, day-to-day action-that-breeds-success knowledge.

She spent more than a decade running her own profitable, award-winning six- figure business and is an expert in micro strategies that lead to increased sales.

Sharon uses her certification in Human Behavior to provide enhanced communication methods to engage and keep clients, boost referrals, and make money.

Her Amazon Best Selling Book: "Legendary Business: From Rats to Riche$" offers practical and easy solutions to five of the most common mistakes business owners make.

By: Sharon Galluzzo

She is married to her college sweetheart and has two daughters. You can often catch Sharon onstage in local community theatre productions. The Galluzzos make their home in North Carolina and love spending time at the beach.

Let me ask you straight out. Are you worth the investment? Is your family worth it? Think about it.

It's been proven that these systems have given us and our clients, more profit, more time with our families, with charities, with travel, with our passions and we want that for YOU too…so remember this: The time is now.

Take action now, right now we'll schedule your Roadmap and our action-takers get the system free as our gift to you!

Just go to www.SharonGalluzzo.com/gift to start today!

CPSIA information can be obtained
at www.ICGtesting.com
Printed in the USA
FSHW011100121019
62956FS